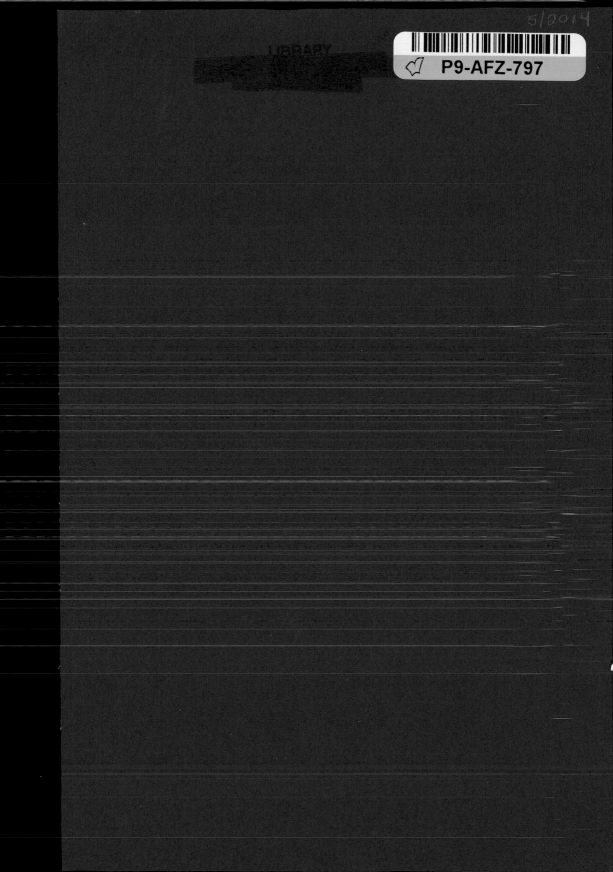

LEAN BUT AGILE

LEAN BUT AGILE

Rethink Workforce Planning and
Gain a True Competitive Edge

William J. Rothwell
James Graber
Neil McCormick

American Management Association

New York • Atlanta • Brussels • Chicago • Mexico City • San Francisco
Shanghai • Tokyo • Toronto • Washington, D.C.

Bulk discounts available. For details visit:
www.amacombooks.org/go/specialsales
Or contact special sales:
Phone: 800-250-5308
E-mail: specialsls@amanet.org
View all the AMACOM titles at: www.amacombooks.org

This publication is designed to provide accurate and authoritative information in regard to the subject matter covered. It is sold with the understanding that the publisher is not engaged in rendering legal, accounting, or other professional service. If legal advice or other expert assistance is required, the services of a competent professional person should be sought.

Library of Congress Cataloging-in-Publication Data

Rothwell, William J., 1951–
   Lean but agile : rethink workforce planning and gain a true competitive edge / William J. Rothwell, James Graber, Neil McCormick.
      p. cm.
   Includes index.
   ISBN-13: 978-0-8144-1777-5 (hbk.)
   ISBN-10: 0-8144-1777-9 (hbk.)
   1. Manpower planning—Cost effectiveness.   2. Personnel management—Cost effectiveness.   3. Strategic planning.   I. Graber, James.   II. McCormick, Neil.   III. Title.

   HF5549.5.M3R6616 2012
   658.3'01—dc23
                                      2011026470

About AMA
American Management Association (www.amanet.org) is a world leader in talent development, advancing the skills of individuals to drive business success. Our mission is to support the goals of individuals and organizations through a complete range of products and services, including classroom and virtual seminars, webcasts, webinars, podcasts, conferences, corporate and government solutions, business books, and research. AMA's approach to improving performance combines experiential learning—learning through doing—with opportunities for ongoing professional growth at every step of one's career journey.

Printing number

10 9 8 7 6 5 4 3 2 1

CONTENTS

PREFACE

FULL-TIME JOBS may be relics of a bygone age, though *work* never seems to go away and, if anything, only becomes more complex. This book is a polemical introduction to a key issue of the day: how to optimize efficient and effective ways to achieve work results in keeping with customer expectations while also minimizing the costly expenses involved in maintaining a cadre of full-time workers.

This issue has been bubbling beneath the surface of workforce issues for a long time. As early as 1994, William Bridges was writing about the "dejobbing of America,"[1] and he predicted that the traditional 9 a.m. to 5 p.m. job would go the way of the dinosaur. More recently employers have continued to look for creative ways to cut costs while maintaining quality service and production. They have tried many ways, such as downsizing; using more contingent workers, contractors, and temporary workers; offshoring; outsourcing; relying on "permanent part-time" staff; relying on teleworkers; and increasing overtime among existing workers. The trouble is that these efforts seem to be approached without any particular rhyme or reason and often do not seem to be driven by any logic other than expediency and a perpetual eagerness to try anything to cut staffing costs.

What is driving this trend toward fundamentally rethinking how work is done? Two words: *cost* and *productivity*. Full-time workers are costly, given their fixed salaries, benefits, and overhead. And they may not be any more productive than part-time workers, consultants, temps, or other ways of staffing to get work done. Consider:

Private industry employers in the United States spent an average of $27.64 per hour
worked for employee compensation in June 2010, according to the U.S. Bureau of Labor
Statistics. Wages and salaries averaged $19.53 per hour worked and accounted for 70.6
percent of these costs, while benefits averaged $8.11 and accounted for the remaining
29.4 percent. Total compensation costs for state and local government workers averaged
$39.74 per hour worked in June 2010. Total compensation costs for civilian workers,
which include private industry and state and local government workers, averaged $29.52
per hour worked in June 2010.[2]

In the United States particularly, employers face double-digit annual increases for health insurance. They are pressured to drive down other costs
and pass on some of these exorbitant health insurance increases to workers
and retirees.

At the same time, employers are experimenting with many ways to get
work done without adding to their full-time payrolls. They are doing that for
many reasons, among them a desire for increased flexibility in how many
people are on the payroll during uncertain economic times, a concern that
full-time workers who do not perform are difficult to fire, a concern that talent needs change so rapidly that hiring full-time workers may actually limit
employer options in whom to tap to get work done, and increasingly fierce
global competition from low-wage nations. James Stoeckmann, senior practice leader at WorldatWork, a professional association of human resources
executives, believes that full-time employees could become the minority of
the U.S. workforce within twenty to thirty years, leaving employees without
traditional benefits—such as health coverage, paid vacations, and retirement plans—that most workers take for granted today. According to Stoeckmann, "The traditional job is not doomed. But it will increasingly have
competition from other models, the most prominent being the independent
contractor model."[3]

This book focuses on the unique issues associated with what we call
Lean but Agile work and workforce planning. By *lean*, we do not mean
"Toyota-style manufacturing methods." Rather, we mean a calculated, systematic effort to plan the work results in keeping with what customers want
and to plan for the workers needed to do the work in timely ways that will
optimize productivity, quality, and cost-effectiveness. By *agile*, we mean
"nimble and fast-moving, positioned to cope with dynamic change." An important goal of the book is to dramatize how important it is to clarify and

focus on measurable, desired outcomes and work backward to design work and staff to achieve those outcomes.

This book consists of eight chapters. Chapter 1 explains what business issues are driving the need for more creative thinking in planning how work is done and how to staff to achieve necessary work results. The chapter also introduces a strategic model for Lean but Agile work and workforce planning.

Chapter 2 is about optimizing work. It makes the case, too often forgotten in books on workforce planning, that the primary goal is to get results, that is, achieve, make products, or offer services that match or exceed customer requirements. How the work is done affects the knowledge, skills, and attitudes needed by workers to achieve those results. We offer suggestions on ways to reengineer work and thereby impact how many and what kind of people are needed to do that work.

Chapter 3 is about building a Lean but Agile workforce. It examines how to build a talent pool that will provide an organization with a lean and agile team.

Chapter 4 is about how to optimize the workforce. How can the best work results be achieved? What range of methods exists to staff for work, and what are their respective advantages and disadvantages?

Chapter 5 is about optimizing the future work and workforce. It offers suggestions for short term and long-term efforts to plan for both work results and the talent necessary to achieve those results.

Chapter 6 is about managing and maintaining lean work and staffing. Traditional methods of management seem antiquated when they are applied to a plethora of approaches to getting the work done and staffing for the work. The chapter examines these issues, offering advice for managers on how to deal with many different, but coexisting, methods of doing the work and staffing for the work.

Chapter 7 explains how to build organizational commitment to Lean but Agile work and staffing, make the business case to senior leaders and other stakeholders for it, clarify the roles and accountabilities of various stakeholder groups, formulate and implement an action plan, communicate about the program to all affected stakeholders, and continually evaluate results.

Chapter 8 offers advice on preparing for the future of lean work and lean workforce planning. It examines future trends and how they may affect the future of work and workforce planning. Additionally, the chapter offers predictions about the future of the contingent workforce globally and some predictions about trends in outsourcing, offshoring, insourcing, and other creative ways to get work done.

The book ends with an appendix from Talent2, the largest HR BPO service provider in the Asia Pacific, describing the HR audit.

William J. Rothwell
State College, Pa., USA

James Graber
Chicago, Ill., USA

Neil McCormick
Brisbane, Queensland, Australia

ACKNOWLEDGMENTS

William J. Rothwell would like to thank his wife, Marcelina, and his daughter, Candice, for just being there for him. Although his son is stuck in the corn-fields of Illinois, Froilan Perucho is not to be forgotten either for just being the wonderful person he is.

James Graber is eternally grateful for the cheerleading provided by his parents, Tom and Doris, and their commitment to writing and sharing knowledge throughout the world. Equivalent thanks are due to Pamela Mary Wolfe, his wife, who always provides support in so many ways. Finally, James hopes for courage, enthusiasm, and agility for daughters Brittany and Grace, who, like others about to enter the workforce, will need to adapt in a world of work where the path forward is less clear than in the past.

Neil McCormick would like to acknowledge the support and input from his colleagues and in particular Dr. Chris Andrews and Richard Boddington and most of all his wife, Debra, for her unwavering belief and support.

We would like to thank the graduate student teams at Penn State University who offered their ideas and help in researching literature and reviewing ideas contained in the book. They are Rashed Alzahmi (team leader), Yasser Binsiddiq, Tutaleni I. Asino (team leader), Jessica Briskin, Michelle Corby (team leader), Woocheol Kim, and Sohel Imroz. Of course, a special thanks to Aileen Zabellero for her excellent project-management skills and her assis-tance as Rothwell's research assistant.

A special thank-you to Christina Parisi, our editor at AMACOM, for her support and patience in helping this book reach the press.

LEAN BUT AGILE

1

AN INTRODUCTION TO LEAN BUT AGILE WORK AND WORKFORCE PLANNING

WHAT IS YOUR ORGANIZATION DOING to hold down employment expenses while simultaneously ensuring that work results meet or exceed customer requirements? How is your organization experimenting with new ways of staffing the work to be done while also achieving the best results? How well is your organization planning systematically for the quantity and quality of people needed to achieve work results in line with customer needs? Read the following vignettes and describe how *your* organization would meet the challenges you find in each. If your organization has ways to solve all of these problems, then perhaps it already has a way to plan comprehensively and systematically for work results and ways for workers to achieve those results. But if your organization cannot solve most of the problems presented here, then your leaders may want to consider a Lean but Agile approach to planning for the work and workforce.

VIGNETTE 1

George Smithers is a top manager in the Acme Corporation. He has just learned that Harold Robbins, one of his most dedicated department managers, will announce his retirement. Smithers is very upset. The reason: He does not believe there is anyone in the company who is qualified to take Robbins's place. Nor does he believe that anyone with Robbins's unique qualifications can be recruited from outside without requiring years of grooming to understand the unique corporate culture of Acme or the special idiosyncrasies of Acme's customers. Smithers has decided to ask the HR department for a succession-planning program before the same problem recurs in other parts of Acme.

VIGNETTE 2

The sales forecast for the Venus Company indicates that sales for company products will drop 40 percent over the next year. At present, staffing expenses—including wages, salary, and benefits—account for 77 percent of company operating expenses. Top managers propose a wholesale, across-the-board 40 percent downsizing to be consistent with the disappointing sales projection. Although the organization is not unionized, top managers feel that the fairest method is to use seniority as the basis for deciding who will be given the axe. That means the last hired will be the first fired.

VIGNETTE 3

A graduate student from a large, well-known university calls the HR department of Vidtronics Corporation and asks to interview the vice president of HR about how the company conducts comprehensive workforce planning. The organization, however, does not conduct comprehensive workforce planning. Instead, decisions are made about whether to fill positions as job vacancies occur. Turnover in the organization has traditionally been quite low, averaging 4 percent or less per year. An analysis of the company's workforce demographics suggests that nearly 40 percent of the top managers and 30 percent of the middle managers will be eligible to retire within the next three years. No effort has thus far been made, however, to address this challenge. The company's executives are discussing whether to launch a succession-planning program.

VIGNETTE 4

The CEO of Electronix Corporation returns from a conference and announces to his senior executive team that a "process improvement effort" should be launched to streamline how the work is done. The CEO heard at the conference that such efforts have successfully reduced workflow problems. The company has one year of unfilled product back orders. The CEO is firmly convinced that a process improvement effort will reduce the back orders by streamlining the production process.

VIGNETTE 5

Top managers of the Vedex Company are worried about the future. They have resisted adding full-time workers to the payroll as sales have increased. The reason: They are uncertain if sales will continue to increase or will decrease, considering the vagaries of a dynamic global economic climate. They prefer to use overtime as a way to staff for meeting work requirements. The HR department reports that during the past year, an average hourly worker in the company clocked two thousand hours of overtime, which means essentially that each full-time worker is putting in about two years of work time for each calendar year. Most are eligible for time-and-a-half overtime pay. The question is whether using overtime is the most cost-effective approach to address the staffing challenge.

VIGNETTE 6

Rhoda Smith is appointed the new vice president of HR in the Windowex Company. She has inherited an HR staff that numbers fifteen people in an organization of two thousand workers. She has been transferred to the job from an operating department in which she has made impressive productivity gains in a short time. The CEO tells her that "HR in this company is broken and needs to be fixed."

Rhoda starts her new job by examining the work records of all the people she has inherited. After doing that, she tells the CEO that her predecessor "must have been drinking when these people were chosen for their jobs, since not one of them has qualifications to match what they have been tasked to do." Most were recruited from within and have never even had one college course or one training program in HR. Rhoda considers how to replace her legacy staff with more qualified people. But she is worried about the need to go through progressive discipline to eliminate the poor performers, which she thinks include most of the staff members she has inherited. She wonders how best to deploy workers, matching individuals appropriately to the work to be done.

Traditional Views of Work Planning and Workforce Planning

As the preceding vignettes illustrate, employers globally are struggling with how to achieve the best work results. Driven by a need to lower costs while increasing productivity, they are not always following traditional ways of planning the work and the workforce. But what are these traditional approaches? What is traditional work planning? What is traditional workforce planning?

Traditional Work Planning

Traditional ways of thinking about planning for work have their roots in the industrial age. An organizational structure (organization chart) is established to allocate responsibilities for various work activities. These activities, in turn, are then broken down further into departments, work groups, jobs, and tasks.

Traditional thinking about work planning emphasizes the work process, that is, how *the work is done*. Little or no attention is devoted to clarifying in detail the measurable work outcomes desired by customers or other stakeholders who care about the work. In some circles, work planning is actually confused with project planning, which is just one way to organize the work to be accomplished. The important point to understand, however, is that the workforce needed to achieve desired work results depends on how the work is done and the desired outcomes. Employers are already experimenting with new ways to get work done. Those experiments affect the workforce needed to achieve work results.

Traditional Workforce Planning

Much has been written about workforce planning in recent years. Indeed, workforce planning has garnered far more attention than has work planning. One reason is that many employers are keenly aware that labor costs are a major expense in doing business. Modern accounting methods treat labor as a cost of doing business while ignoring the critical importance of human creative talent as the only active ingredient that can serve as a catalyst to add value to land, finances, technology, or other assets.

Traditional workforce planning follows the logic of economics. As demand for products or services increases, it creates a demand for labor to make the products or deliver the services. *Labor demand* refers to the quantity and quality of people needed to meet production or service delivery requirements. *Labor supply* refers to the quantity and quality of people currently employed by the organization. As labor demand increases as a function of production or service demand, more people are needed to meet the demand. In short, a larger supply of people is needed.

But this relationship is not precise. Sometimes the number of workers affects productivity directly. In other cases, such as managerial work, managers can oversee increasing employees until a tipping point is reached. To complicate matters, sometimes the quality of workers affects productivity. A few talented people may outperform an army.

The traditional approach to workforce planning, based in economics, has some distinct disadvantages. The first disadvantage is that future labor demand is forecasted based on past experience. In short, economists tend to assume that the same quantity and quality of people will be needed to achieve future results as were needed to achieve past results. Unfortunately, technology and other productivity breakthroughs can actually change the quantity and quality of people needed in the future. The second disadvantage is that economists struggle with the notion of differences in individual talent. Not all people are equally productive, or even equally productive in the same ways. Some people are simply more productive than others, and talents—understood to mean *personal strengths* in this context—differ on an individual basis. Some research suggests that the difference between the average and the most productive worker can be as high as eleven times.

Many methods are available to conduct workforce planning. They are drawn from quantitatively focused approaches from statistics, econometrics, or operations research and from qualitatively focused approaches to problem solving. Few organizations undertake any form of systematic, comprehensive workforce planning. In fact, one study found that as many as two-thirds of U.S. employers do no comprehensive workforce planning.[1] Instead, jobs are typically approved in many organizations on a case-by-case basis as vacancies become available or as work demand increases. The result: The collective competencies and talents of the entire organization's workforce is never assessed against the requirements needed to achieve the organization's strategic goals. The result is that the labor force of many organizations can drift away over time from the best fit to achieve desired work results.

A New Approach to Workforce Planning

A review of changing conditions in business over the past sixty years provides an important backdrop for understanding the need for change in many business practices. The years from 1950 to 1970 were a golden age of business stability for industrialized nations. Human resources practices were designed to be responsive to those conditions. Building a stable workforce was the priority. As detailed by Peter Cappelli,[2] the following conditions prevailed:

- Business demand and the talent needed to deliver it could be accurately predicted into the future.

- Government regulations restricted competition, which helped companies confidently make long-term investments. Foreign competition was often almost nonexistent or held very low market share.

- Competitors operated in unison. When GM announced its price increases, Chrysler and Ford were sure to follow.

- Union contracts across industries resulted in similar labor expenses and in large part removed the variable of price advantages.

- Talent was in short supply and could not be easily found or lured away from the competition.

- The economy grew steadily, at 5 to 6 percent per year.

During World War II in the United States the War Planning Commission required companies to report on their current and future staffing needs to minimize the chance that the war effort would be hampered by product shortages. This practice continued after the war. By the 1960s, 96 percent of organizations reported having a dedicated talent-management function. Workforce planning thrived. Companies could accurately project their business trajectory as well as their talent needs years in advance. Therefore, organizations could justify ambitious, ten-year-long management-development programs.

By the early 1970s, business conditions began to change. Deregulation, more rapid technology development, and greater foreign competition all reduced stability. More competition and improved technology led to faster product development cycles; five to ten years to bring out a new product line was no longer required. Increasingly, there was insufficient time to develop worker skills internally when changes in products and strategies were often faster than the time it would take for companies to retool current employees. Meanwhile, the talent shortages after World War II were remedied as external recruiting firms became prevalent, able to supply talent from outside the organization.

Mergers, acquisitions, and divesting of "non-core businesses" led to more turmoil in human resources and talent-management practices. Inevitably, mergers and acquisitions led to downsizing to gain efficiencies by reducing duplicative talent. During a merger or an acquisition, voluntary turnover often increases, which means that talent developed at great expense exits. Job ladders are broken, as are individual career paths, as business strategies change and firms are restructured. In an environment of frequent mergers and acquisitions, the mentality may be that it is not worth investing in human resources development when inherited talent is unknown and unproven. Divestiture of non-core businesses also leads to unpredictability, a bane of human resources planning.

In 1973 and 1974, the OPEC oil embargo delivered a blow to stability as it drove up commodity prices critical to the global economy. Inflation gathered steam. Then came the 1981 recession, the worst at the time since the Great Depression, and in the United States there was a 2 percent reduction in GDP. With the recession there was suddenly a glut of talent. Several years later, an improving economy did not mean a return to the old ways. Emphasis on cutting costs continued, and downsizing increased every year from 1990 to 1996 in the United States, even though the economy during this period was expanding. Job cuts were as great in 1993–1995, during a good period, as during the deep recession of 1901–1903.[3] After the year 2000, there were periods of talent shortage as well as periods of very deep layoffs, as world economies experienced both great booms and an even greater recession than that of 1981–1983.

Work planning, like workforce planning, has also been negatively impacted by changes in the business climate after 1970. Management by Objectives (MBO) and similar work-planning programs were initiated beginning in the 1950s and remain prevalent today. Annually, organizations plan the objectives for the next year and then cascade them down through the hierarchy of the organization to focus the efforts of all employees on key performance indicators. The process can take several months in a larger organization. Clearly, planning of this type benefits from a stable environment where it is not necessary to change direction frequently. It is not designed to be flexible and responsive to environmental needs. There is little or no provision in traditional MBO or other performance-planning programs to initiate a new planning process midyear when conditions and priorities change. Instead, in light of the large scope of effort work planning requires as well as bonuses being linked to the annual objectives, companies typically feel committed to plow forward with the plan as is. Thus, the annual plan can result in a lack of responsiveness and lost time and can also undermine faith in leadership.

This review of the challenges to planning in an unstable environment is not meant to suggest that planning today is fruitless and impossible and should therefore be jettisoned along with any other waste of time and resources. In fact, in light of the heightened need to marshal resources wisely, it is more important than ever for organizations to clearly focus on what results they are trying to achieve and map out the work and workforces they need to get there. But today, organizations need to plan for instability, which requires that they not overcommit resources and that they develop mechanisms that allow them to move quickly in new directions. That is, organizations must strive to be Lean but Agile.

Today's Priority: Increasing Performance, Cutting Costs

The authors collectively work with clients on five continents. It is difficult to find an organization today where workers do not perceive their organizations as "lean" in their staffing, particularly the old-timers who recall how organizations were structured thirty or forty years ago. Similarly, budgets and other resources are constrained. "Doing more with less" is an all too familiar refrain. The organizational imperatives for survival today are:

- *Organizations must prepare themselves to handle the "unpredictability" of the business environment.* They must be able to change direction rapidly based on customer demands, competitor strategies, innovation, pricing, or regulatory changes. Companies may not be able to recover from an overcommitment to any single strategy.

- *Companies must develop a good solution to manage the "unpredictability" of talent needs.* Too much talent leads to costly and morale-damaging layoffs and restructuring. Too little talent leads to talent shortages. Now is the time to assume uncertainty of talent need and develop good ways to manage that uncertainty.

- *Companies must have a nearly obsessive focus on controlling costs and leveraging resources wisely if they do not want to be surpassed by competitors.* Customers have more choice of providers than ever before as well as improved means to easily find and compare the competition, and monopolies are on the wane.

Today there is need for an approach that allows the work as well as the workforce to change rapidly as dictated by circumstances, to deal better with changes that *cannot be accurately predicted* in today's business environment. Lean but Agile is a strategy for being both very agile in responding to change (or risk becoming quickly irrelevant) and adept at leveraging scarce resources wisely (lean). Many organizations have already begun the journey, but almost all have room to advance the practice of Lean but Agile further.

The Three Principles of Lean but Agile

Three fundamental principles guide the practice of Lean but Agile. These may seem obvious and even elementary, and yet the words of Benjamin Franklin, the eighteenth-century U.S. statesman and scientist, were never more appropriate: "You will observe with Concern how long a useful Truth may be known, and exist, before it is generally receiv'd and practis'd on."[4] The principles are:

1. *Focus on strategic/high-impact work.* This is the oft-forgotten principle. Why would organizations pay large sums for nonessential work? There is little point in optimizing the workforce to do work that is not really essential to implement organizational strategy, achieve organizational goals, and leverage a firm's competitive advantages. A surprisingly large percentage of work (more than half) done in most organizations is not essential to the mission.[5] Further, work may be tied to the mission but be of low impact. Understanding the work means ensuring that it flows from organizational strategy or objectives, translating it into performance goals and metrics, and clearly communicating all this to workers. It also means specifying and documenting work processes and the time and resources required to complete the work. Specifying and documenting the work helps to get and keep workers up to speed quickly on what is important. Chapter 2 will describe how to identify essential work.

2. *Build a talent pool.* It is striking to consider how little most organizations know about their workforces, and yet this information is critical for deploying them wisely. If you do not understand the talents as well as the as-

sociated costs of your current workforce and talent pool, you cannot identify the resources with the best return on investment for an assignment or, more generally, optimize workforce use. Chapter 3 describes talent pools in detail.

3. *Use alternative work sources.* This rule could also be stated as "staff up with full-time employees to meet minimum work demand but rely on alternative workers to meet maximum demand." It is widely understood that full-time employees are expensive and are a fixed cost. Success at transforming employees to a more variable cost has been very limited because the variable percentage of compensation (the portion at risk) is typically small, particularly on the downside, and because of costs associated with employment termination. And yet varying work demand is almost inevitable for all business, if for no other reason than the peaks and valleys of the economy. Even when overall work demand is stable, many organizations have cyclical demand, such as retailers during the holiday season. In chapter 4 we discuss a broad array of alternative work arrangements available to organizations.

In chapter 5 we cover optimizing the future work and workforce. Chapter 6 explores managing and maintaining lean work and staffing. Chapter 7 explains how to build organizational commitment to Lean but Agile work and staffing, make the business case to senior leaders and other stakeholders for it, clarify the roles and accountabilities of various stakeholder groups, formulate and implement an action plan, communicate about the program to all affected stakeholders, and continuously evaluate results. Chapter 8 examines future trends and how they may affect the future of work and workforce planning.

The Need for a Lean but Agile Approach to Work Planning and Workforce Planning

The time has come for many organizations to consider a Lean but Agile approach to work planning and workforce planning. But what is meant by "lean" and "agile"? What is meant by "Lean but Agile work planning" and "Lean but Agile workforce planning"?

What Is *Lean*?

Lean is as much philosophy as it is approach. The basic idea is to increase or enhance customer value while reducing waste. While first popularized by

Toyota and later by other manufacturers in so-called lean manufacturing, lean thinking can be applied in any type of organization—private, public, or nonprofit.

What Is *Agile*?

Agile means nimble. An agile organization can staff up quickly to meet unexpected challenges and staff down quickly when demand declines for products or services. When most workers are employed full-time, the organization has limited agility and must take steps like downsizing when demand declines. The reverse is also true: when needs suddenly surface, as in the case of an emergency or a crisis, the organization must take steps to staff up quickly. That is not always easy.

What Is *Lean but Agile Work Planning*?

Lean but Agile work planning is a philosophy as well as an approach. It begins with the assumption that the most important thing to do is to clarify what measurable, observable product or service requirements must be achieved to meet or exceed customer expectations while also preserving the ability to anticipate or react quickly to dynamic demands. From there the organization's leaders and workers work backward to pinpoint methods to achieve those desired product or service goals. Work is examined according to questions such as these:[6]

- What are the desired, measurable work outputs that are essential to meet or exceed customer or stakeholder expectations or needs?

- What feedback systems are critical to ensure that the work results meet or exceed customer or stakeholder expectations or needs?

- How should the work processes be most efficiently and effectively carried out?

- What work inputs are essential to carrying out the work?

- How can the organization react with maximum speed to changing threats and opportunities?

When these questions are asked, the organization's leaders and workers may have to rethink fundamentally what work is done, how it is done, and how successful results (as determined by customers or stakeholders) are achieved and made measurable.

What Is *Lean but Agile Workforce Planning*?

Lean but Agile workforce planning is also a philosophy and an approach. It examines the human side of achieving the desired outputs over time. It poses such questions as:

- *Who* is best able to achieve the desired outputs?
- *What* will the people do to carry out the work processes?
- *When* are the work results needed at various stages of production or service delivery, and how will that affect the timing when human talents are needed?
- *Where* are the work results needed at various stages of production or service delivery, and how will that affect the human talents needed?
- *How* can the work results be best achieved, and how will that affect the human talents needed?
- *What are the advantages and disadvantages* (costs and benefits) of various approaches to getting the work done and achieving desired work results?
- *How can the maximum speed* be obtained in matching the quantity and quality of staffing to work demands?

When these questions are asked, the organization's leaders and workers may have to fundamentally rethink the quantity and quality of people needed to achieve measurable results of competitive advantage to the organization. All assumptions about previous working relationships are fundamentally brought into question. It is not, for example, assumed that a "permanent, full-time workforce" is necessarily needed to address the questions raised above. Indeed, many different approaches may be used to staff how work results are achieved. For instance, an organization may establish a "zero-based talent-management strategy" in which managers at all levels must justify the continuation of each worker each year based on business needs.

Distinguishing Lean but Agile Work and Workforce Planning from Related Topics

Terms can be confusing if they are not carefully explained. That is especially true for terms such as succession planning, succession management, and talent management. Therefore, it is worth devoting some time to clarifying what these terms mean.

Succession Planning

Succession planning is usually understood to mean developing people from inside the organization to meet future staffing needs. Although some succession plans may be limited to an organization's top leaders (that is, the CEO and his or her direct reports), they do not need to be. In fact, succession plans may be devised to groom talent for any position in an organization.

Lean but Agile work planning means organizing what work is done and how it is done to achieve the best measurable results. *Lean but Agile workforce planning* means determining the quantity and quality of people needed by an organization to achieve its strategic objectives over time. While succession planning focuses on the existing staff members of an organization and efforts to prepare them systematically for future challenges, lean work and workforce planning focus on what work is to be done; how it will be organized; how it will be effectively matched to customer needs; and how it can be done to minimize the expenditures of time, money, and effort.

Succession Management

Succession management is usually understood to mean daily efforts to develop people from inside the organization to meet future staffing needs. Instead of relying on annual, semiannual, quarterly, or monthly talent review meetings and a strategic framework to put in place programs meant to develop people for future challenges, succession management is inherently tactical, that is, what managers do on a daily basis to prepare people for the future.

Lean but Agile work and workforce planning may also be thought of as having strategic and tactical elements. *Strategic work planning* examines how to organize the work over time to achieve the best measurable outcomes; *strategic workforce planning* examines how to plan comprehensively for matching the best configuration of the quantity and quality of people to do the work and achieve the desired work results. *Tactical work planning* means how to organize work tasks on a daily or project basis; *tactical work-force planning* means staffing specific tasks or assignments to get the most efficient (do things right) and effective (do the right things) results.

Talent Management

While *talent management* has sometimes seemed like a term in search of a definition, most people would agree that it basically means systematic efforts to integrate the ways to attract, develop, deploy, and retain the most productive and promotable people. It thus goes beyond succession planning by including recruitment, selection, onboarding, and retention as well as development.

Lean but Agile work and workforce planning are actually larger and more comprehensive issues than talent management. Instead of focusing on the best people, Lean but Agile workforce planning looks at *all* the people (both quantity and quality) an organization needs over time to achieve results. And Lean but Agile work planning looks at how the work is organized in *inputs* (cues and resource requirements necessary), *conditions* (governing factors such as reporting relationship), *process steps* (how the work is to be done), *outputs* (desired, measurable results), *consequences* (value-added features), and *feedback* (information provided by others during and after the results are delivered).[7]

There is an overlap between talent management and Lean but Agile in their interest in deployment. Are the right people in the right places at the right times to achieve the right results? Although that has not been a particular focus of attention for many talent-management programs, it is essential to Lean but Agile thinking.

Making the Case for Lean but Agile Work and Workforce Planning

Organizational leaders today increasingly find that they cannot afford to sustain a huge, so-called permanent workforce of full-time workers. Instead, they are driven by considerations of cost and productivity to formulate other approaches. Unfortunately, most of the creative alternatives they come up with are not driven by systematic approaches. Instead, managers experiment with many approaches to get results. Those that work out—or seem to work out better than expected—are prone to overuse. Managers simply have no systematic way to consider a slate of alternatives strategically or tactically to get the work done.

It is clear that much experimentation is under way. Some organizations experiment with temporary, contingent, contract, or consulting talent to get much work accomplished; some experiment with new approaches to performing the work; some rely on overtime, part-time help, outsourcing, or offshoring; and some try using retirees or other nontraditional workforces (such as teleworkers or flex place workers) to get results. The approaches used are dazzlingly diverse. But they do not seem to be driven by any rational framework. Many managers would welcome some guidance on what approaches to use in getting the work done and/or in staffing to get that work done. And that is exactly the problem that Lean but Agile work and workforce planning is meant to solve.

A Strategic Model to Guide Lean but Agile Work and Workforce Planning

Most organizations find that a road map of some kind will be helpful in guiding their efforts to formulate, implement, and sustain a Lean but Agile work and workforce planning effort. Such models can be *strategic* (comprehensive) or *tactical* (situational or focused on specific work tasks/positions). A strategic model to guide Lean but Agile work and workforce planning is depicted in Figure 1-1. A description of it follows.

Figure 1-1: A Strategic Model to Guide Lean but Agile Work and Workforce Planning

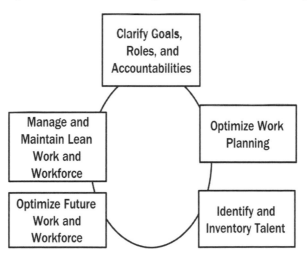

Step 1: Clarify Goals, Roles, and Accountabilities

The first step is to clarify why the organization is undertaking Lean but Agile work and workforce planning and what measurable results are desired from it. That involves clarifying goals. Senior leaders should agree on those goals.

Possible goals might include:

- Cutting operating expenses
- Slashing labor costs
- Reducing waste
- Increasing customer or stakeholder satisfaction
- Reducing cycle time to get the work accomplished
- Reacting more quickly to changing competitive conditions
- Matching the right human talents to business requirements in a more timely fashion

Begin by raising possible goals for leaders to consider. Then urge them to establish a baseline (a measurable starting point) and pinpoint targets for the goals they have agreed upon. Feedback systems will be needed to gather data from customers or other stakeholders to ensure that results are monitored over time.

Next, leaders should agree on who does what to achieve the goals. That will require clarification of the roles of:

- The CEO
- The top management team
- The HR department
- Each operating manager
- Each worker

Finally, what are the accountabilities? How will each group with a role be held accountable for enacting its respective roles and helping the organization achieve its goals? Will accountability be established by rewards for measurable targets achieved, by punishment for failure to achieve measurable targets, or some other way of ensuring that people are held accountable?

Step 2: Optimize Work Planning

Do not assume that the work will be performed as usual or that business will be conducted as usual. Begin by asking, *"What measurable results do customers or other stakeholders really need from this organization, and what role does each part of the organization—and each individual in the organization—play in achieving the desired, measurable results?"* A corollary to that question is *"What does our organization do better than any other?"* For the whole organization, identify the work outputs offered to external customers and stakeholders. Then poll customers and other stakeholders to determine exactly—in measurable and observable terms—what they would like to see in work results. How do customers define a good product? How do other external stakeholders define good results? What will it take to meet or exceed these requirements now and in the future? How can the organization leverage what it does best?

Then repeat the process for each part of the organization. What work outputs result from the actions of each organizational part? How do stakeholders—that is, those who care about those results—define a good work result? How closely do the existing work outputs of each part of the organization measure up to those desired results?

It is also possible to repeat the process for each worker within the organization. What key performance indicators or targets are desired from each worker? How can they be achieved? What behaviors should desirably be linked to those results?

Step 3: Identify and Inventory Talent

In this step, explore the full range of talent available in the organization. Does everyone contribute the same to meeting or exceeding customer or stakeholder expectations? That is most unlikely. So who does the best job of meeting or exceeding customer/stakeholder expectations? Who contributes most to the essence of what makes the organization competitive, and precisely what do they contribute? Exactly what does the organization do that makes it successful in the eyes of customers or other stakeholders? What unique characteristics do these individuals possess, and how could they be described for purposes of finding that talent within the whole organization? One way to describe these characteristics is as "competencies," that is, any characteristic of a human being that leads to average or superior results.

The notion of "talent" is a debatable one. Some experts limit the definition of talent to those who are both promotable and performing their current jobs well (so-called High Potentials). Other experts define talent as unique individual strengths. Still other experts define talent as those who possess specialized knowledge of value to the organization (so-called High Potentials). Another way to think about it is that everyone has the opportunity to become "talented"—meaning "being especially good at something"—if he or she devotes at least ten thousand hours of skilled practice and effort to it.[8]

Step 4: Optimize Future Work and Workforce

The future will not be the same as the past. Every day new technology introduces opportunities to change work results. Every day, customers may change their minds about what they regard as good or exceptional work results. (Think for a moment about how people think of cell phones now compared to their opinions of what was a good cell phone five years ago.) Changing notions of acceptable or superior work can affect the measurable results to be achieved and the kind of human talents needed to achieve those results.

Step 5: Manage and Maintain a Lean but Agile Work and Workforce

Managing and maintaining "Lean but Agile work planning" and "Lean but Agile workforce planning" will mean that leaders—and workers—must adapt, often quickly, to changing customer and stakeholder expectations, new ways of working, and new competencies needed to do the work. Traditional notions of management that treat everyone the same will have to be reconsidered from a Lean but Agile perspective. The goal will be to achieve results in line with customer and stakeholder expectations. However, what has to be done (the work) and who will do it (the workforce) will necessarily change. That means managers themselves will have to be Lean but Agile to keep up with increasingly complex ways of working and staffing.

Chapter Summary

This chapter provided a background on traditional views of work and workforce planning. It explained that traditional ways of thinking about planning for work have their roots in the industrial age and that the organizational chart is established to allocate responsibilities for various work activities. Moreover, traditional thinking about work planning emphasizes the *work process*, that is, how the work is done. Traditional workforce planning is based on the views of economists, who reduce human beings to "supplies" and "demands" to meet organizational production or service delivery needs. Unfortunately, few organizations undertake any comprehensive and systematic approach to work or workforce planning. Instead, they deal with staffing needs on a case-by-case basis.

A new approach is needed to plan for work and workforce needs. It is based on lean thinking, which emphasizes meeting or exceeding customer requirements while also decreasing waste. Add to that idea the view that it must be fast but good, which speaks to agility. Lean but Agile work planning begins by clarifying what work products or services are desired by customers or other stakeholders. Lean but Agile workforce planning looks at the most efficient and effective ways to staff to make those products or deliver those services.

This chapter also described a strategic model to integrate strategic Lean but Agile work and workforce planning. The key steps in the strategic lean work planning and workforce planning model are (1) clarify goals, roles, and accountabilities; (2) optimize work planning; (3) identify and inventory talent; (4) optimize future work and workforce; and (5) manage and maintain lean work and workforce.

CHAPTER 2

OPTIMIZE THE WORK

TO DELIVER A SUCCESSFUL Lean but Agile program we need to ensure that the foundation of the program is sound. To that end this chapter investigates the need to focus on organizational strategic objectives in both the near and long term. This chapter also investigates the need to understand what work must be completed at an organizational and functional level, including the critical nature of those functional requirements. It also examines the capability required to deliver the designated work. To ensure that these foundational components are sound, we discuss the need for rigor and repeatability in the way organizational leaders review and/or audit information, data, and activity. We also discuss the latest benchmarks to measure against. To frame a Lean but Agile program we begin with a general discussion on Outcome-Based Management (OM) and the Outcome Management Framework (OMF) of input, process, output, and outcome that supports it.

The OMF, when applied to human resources activities, can sharpen the focus of those engaged in work and workforce planning to help achieve Lean but Agile work and workforce planning. To deliver an optimized work model using the OMF, it is necessary to link the organizational strategic objectives with the human capital needed to achieve them. A framework is needed to

Optimize the Work 21

structure how to design, analyze, monitor, and fine-tune to deliver optimal outcomes. For this purpose OM and the OMF are discussed and illustrated.

Outcome Management and the Outcome Management Framework

OM is a strategic approach to ensure that initiatives are designed around planned outcomes. There is also an ongoing measurement of how well the intended outcomes are being achieved, with feedback loops to inform decisions on the potential need to adjust goals. To establish a successful outcome management process, decision makers must refocus and redefine success in outcome-based terms. OM systems are therefore used to set objectives and performance indicators to focus on outcomes and organizational results. OM systems then measure those results to enhance an organization's ability to provide services that effectively achieve goals. OM can inform management decisions about ways to allocate resources and deliver services.

The OMF is a planning and management approach to guide the formulation of outcomes to achieve the desired organizational strategic objectives. OMF is focused on *why things are done*. The focus of the latter is on *purpose* rather than on just *process* or *process improvement* alone. Together these two approaches can enable organizations to avert daily crisis management to some extent by engaging in long-term work and workforce planning, especially in tight economic times.

The OMF forms the foundation of a Lean but Agile program as illustrated in the following examples.

Example 2-1: Objectives, Inputs, Processes, Outputs, and Outcomes

Imagine that the leaders of an organization want to improve overall profitability (*the objective*) and decide to do so by increasing the percentage of sales leads, which is to result in more orders (*the outcome*). The HR department is contacted to initiate a development program to improve individual performance in getting leads. This improvement is *the output*.

HR dutifully rolls out a training program. *The inputs* for the program include the trainers, the sales personnel, the tools and equipment used, and the funds required. The actual training program is *the process*. The results of the training, measured by scores and score improvement, are *the output*. If the *output* does not deliver the targeted *outcome*, the program/project is deemed a failure. Hence, the imperative must be to measure activities for outcomes continually throughout the process.

Example 2-2: A Ride to Paris

Take a group of cyclists heading for Paris from Lyon. They are so entrenched in achieving their *outputs* (covering thirty miles per day) they miss the turn to Paris at Nevers and head for Bordeaux instead. While they will continue to achieve their *output* of thirty miles per day, they will never achieve the targeted *outcome*—reaching Paris.

Significant work has been undertaken in the public sector in recent years developing and evolving the concepts and practice of Outcome-Based Management. One example of the use of this approach is the Victorian Auditor General (VAG) (2010) report "Performance Reporting by Departments."[1] This report highlighted the lack of explicit linkage to the outcomes of many departmental activities. Organizations can benefit from these developments through OM, particularly since its focus is improvement in productivity and service delivery. The focus of OM is on the outcome required to deliver on the organization's strategic objectives.

A Lean but Agile Program and Human Resources Activity

We have highlighted the origins of a Lean but Agile program and explained how OM is its foundation.

When we apply the program's framework to human resources activity we gain a further perspective. In many circumstances, this activity is focused on processes to deliver outputs while orchestrating inputs. Thus, HR activity becomes output-oriented, although the activity itself is not focused on outcome (see Figures 2-1 and 2-2). This, in turn, leads to a tactical focus that in most instances ignores the overall organizational objective.

If you only focus on processes and/or outputs, you can never tell whether you have been effective or whether you are providing "value for money" services. HR departments without explicit strategic objectives are then likely to operate at a tactical or transactional level, and can only ever evaluate transactional effectiveness. They may be valued, but the impact value of HR activities cannot be evaluated.[2]

Figure 2-1 and Figure 2-2 compare the typical focus of human resources activity to the focus when a Lean but Agile program is in place.

Figure 2-1: Typical Focus of Human Resources Activity

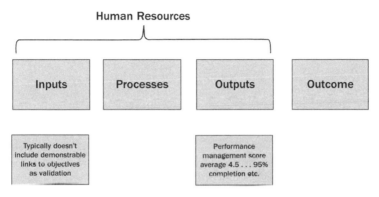

Figure 2-2: Lean but Agile Work and Workforce Planning Framework

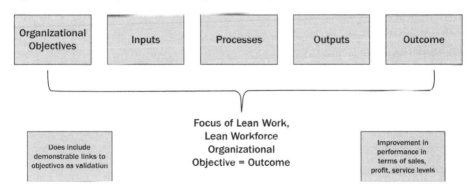

Start with an Environmental Scan

While this chapter deals with optimizing work, this activity is best undertaken when there is a solid understanding of the organization's current situation in achieving the existing targeted *objectives and outcomes, inputs, processes,* and *outputs.* An "environmental scan," an internal and external assessment of the organization's business environment, can prepare the way for meaningful communication and assist in the initial strategy design for optimizing work. (Further detail regarding an environmental scan can be found in chapter 5.) To achieve the rigor needed to evaluate the organization's current situation and plan for the future, there needs to be consistency in how activities are assessed, how they are measured, and how they are described. This is, at times, quite challenging.

Challenges to Optimizing Work

The challenge facing those managing work and workforce designs and planning is their ability to influence work decisions *before* those decisions are actionable. It is critical to gain a detailed understanding of organizational strategic objectives, the work required to deliver these objectives, the feasibility of meeting them, and the potential machinations along the way if organizations are to move away from the typical "crisis management" of daily activity.

The Lack of Consistent Terminology

Another significant issue in work planning is the lack of consistency in terminology, processes, and measures as well as the metrics used to define success. Definitions of such terms as *strategic, tactical,* and *critical* can vary. Few organizations use terms consistently.

To begin to achieve a consistent understanding of the language and its linkages to organizational strategic objectives and work requirements, a framework needs to be used that links organizational strategic objectives to the human capital required to attain those objectives. This can be seen in Figure 1-1 in chapter 1.

A first step in this process is the creation of a common language. As the analysis is undertaken it is critical to also include:

- A repeatable way to measure,
- A standard to measure against, and
- A range of metrics to compare against.

Terminology, Measurement, and Activity Standards

Globally, efforts are under way to address this shortfall in consistent, rigorous terminology. In the United States, headway is being made to standardize the terminology through the current standards project of the Society for Human Resource Management (SHRM). Additionally, the global financial crisis has focused analysts' attention on the need to compare the state of human capital management within corporations. To that end, OrcaEyes Inc. Human Capital Indices have been created, covering some fifty-seven criteria. Global activity in this regard outside of the United States is also significant. Human resources standards are under development in Europe, Singapore, Australia, New Zealand, and elsewhere.

Further initiatives include the creation of reliable, defensible, and repeatable ways to measure human resources activity. A human resources performance audit has been developed based on the work of Dr. Chris Andrews, human resources director at Queensland's Bond University in Australia, in his thesis "Developing and Conducting a Human Resource Management Performance Audit: Case Study of an Australian University."[3] Andrews further extended this audit development to measure human resources activity in the commercial sector. An example of the human resources audit process is described in the appendix.

These human resources performance audit and review developments now render HR activity measurable. Early work by the Higher Education Funding Council for England (HEFCE) in the creation of higher education human resources standards[4] was further developed in conjunction with twenty-one universities as part of a workforce productivity program funded by the Australian federal government for the improvement of workforce productivity in higher education.[5] The standards include measures for criteria assessed and they focus on learning and development, performance management, attraction and recruitment, workforce planning, and remuneration and benefits. Additionally, associated consulting models and frameworks have been developed.

How to Use the Standards and Review Processes

The HR standards discussed here have been designed to align with the HR performance audit framework. The premise of each standard is: "What would someone expect to see in a function that was performing well?" The structure of the standards follows the OMF where the outcome equals the organizational objective.

Workforce Planning Standards

The workforce planning standard shown at http://www.hrd.qut.edu.au/ hrbenchmarking/wpp.jsp is an example of how to apply Outcome-Based Management. Additionally, by taking the included workforce planning standards and applying what is specifically high value/high risk for the organization, a template can be quickly created of what workforce planning should look like in that organization, including what *inputs, processes, outputs,* and *outcomes* are expected to be seen and what metrics and processes should be measured.

In working with this adjusted standard and reviewing—if indeed these inputs, processes, outputs, and outcomes are being delivered, or even exist—the process equates to a review of these functions. Even the most complex functions can be reviewed in mere days. The results of the review will provide a blueprint for necessary enhancements.

Crisis Management

The dynamic demands of modern work organizations are forcing many leaders to abandon the notion of work and workforce planning beyond their immediate needs. Typically, this means the focus is firmly fixed on the next budget or reporting period. Research indicates that more than 66 percent of U.S. organizations do not have detailed workforce plans. Most workforce activity is driven by expediency. A key reason is that HR managers and line managers must focus on solving immediate human capital problems.

Moving from Crisis Management

Today crisis management in human capital appears to be more the norm than the exception. It can be a major time waster. In daily business, the majority of what we see described as work planning or "strategic" activity is, in reality, crisis management in disguise.

Human resources services are typically under constant pressure to solve immediate problems and meet immediate needs, so they are focused on addressing a current crisis or achieving the next milestone. But rarely do they possess the resources, methodologies, and strategies to get above the "noise" of the current crisis. (To state it in the colorful terms of one client, "We are too busy fighting off the crocodiles to drain the swamp.")

We are not suggesting that efforts to meet immediate needs be replaced. There is, however, a far better way to support these tactical decisions and to develop strategies to reach long-term objectives and adjust to meet urgent daily needs.

What we are offering in *Lean but Agile* is a way to move beyond the daily crises and focus on the end goal, the avoidance of such crises, and in turn the achievement of organizational strategic objectives. The following analogy is intended to illustrate the advantage of developing a workforce plan using a Lean but Agile program.

Example 2-3: Climbing the Eiger

Imagine for a moment a mountain-climbing team is about to embark on an attempt to scale the Eiger mountain in Switzerland. The team splits into two groups. The first group sets off with, at best, a vague idea of how to get to the top. Its focus is on getting everyone moving, so the group members just start climbing without a clear plan. They want to get to the top in the shortest possible time. They climb well until they discover they need a bridging mechanism but do not have one. This creates the first crisis, and team members are sent down the mountain to collect one (if one is available). The delay causes consternation, so more pressure is applied to move faster when they resume climbing. The team members then make good progress, climbing superbly and achieving their hourly climb rate. Their total concentration on each step and each yard ahead to maintain the hourly climb rate causes them to choose the easiest and quickest ascent path rather than slow down somewhat to traverse a ridge leading to the summit. Because the immediate pressure is to climb faster, they lose the orientation of where they are heading. They do not realize that they have missed the turn to the peak and have charged off in the wrong direction. That presents another crisis. Now they have to backtrack. When they finally get back on course, the last crisis is the "clincher." They discover that a team member needs to free-climb around a major overhang to secure ropes for the rest of the team to make the final ascent. This is a very specialized skill. A check of the team indicates that no member possesses the necessary skills. They cannot source the skills, so their climb comes to an abrupt halt. They fail to reach the summit.

In contrast, the second group studies the best strategy to reach the top of the Eiger, all the way from the base camp to the peak, before starting the climb. With their objective in mind, the group members "backtrack" from the summit to the base camp to devise a workable plan. First they check the viability of achieving this goal. Is this group capable of reaching the summit? Should they reevaluate what is achievable? They note the potential pitfalls along the way and the tools and skills needed for the climb. They recognize that they do not possess all the skills necessary to achieve the objective, and they secure climbers with those skills before the skills are needed.

The second group discovers obstacles, some major, along the way. But its members have mapped out each step and each directional change with full awareness of where and what their objective is at each segment of the climb and what they can anticipate later on. Before their departure they are aware, for instance, that the bridging mechanism will be needed only for two-thirds of the climb, but they will then need free climbers, climbing rope, and pinions. They plan to jettison the excess load of the bridging mechanism, using ropes and pinions in a timely fashion.

We know who achieves the objective (the summit) and can easily understand why.

If we apply such an analogy to a common human capital management scenario, we can see some striking similarities to the first group's efforts:

- How often do organizations articulate goals in terms of aspirations rather than specific deliverables?
- Is there any realistic assessment that the objective can be achieved?
- Is an effort made to define what success looks like before trying to achieve an objective?
- Is an effort made to create a path from the objective, the "future state," back to today?

By continually looking back to today from a clearly defined future position (the *objective*) we can see how decisions made today will affect the achievement of the desired objective and adjust today's decisions accordingly.

It is absolutely critical that the focus of the journey is the next step. In the business world this may be the next reporting period, the next week, or next month in the calendar year. However, if the objective does not receive proper attention, then great strides may be made but could lead to progress in the wrong direction. On the other hand, if too much attention is paid to the final objective and due care is not taken to concentrate on current needs, all will be at risk. According to our analogy, that could mean walking straight off the side of the mountain or completely missing the mark in reaching an objective. There needs to be a balance between daily activity and the long-range view in any Lean but Agile program. Creating a future strategy will direct tactical delivery of HR services, and the results of this tactical delivery will in turn inform, and potentially change, future strategy. There cannot be two paths, just one path with a focus on tactical delivery of outcomes informed by the requirements of the final objective.

If there is a lack of focus on the final objective, however, the concentration of effort is always going to be tactical and related to the crisis of the day or the next milestone, without reference to the final objective. This shortsighted approach causes many organizations to constantly change direction as the next crisis unfolds. This can, in turn, breed change fatigue in the workforce, making the efforts needed to move from one direction to another more difficult. Even the most efficient, effective, and economic human resources department can only serve as crisis managers in this scenario.

To continually review the current requirements with the future objective firmly in the design, not just the next milestone, is to gain a deeper understanding of what human resources requirements will be necessary to achieve the overall objective. This understanding has the potential to radically change the complexity of the requirements of the workforce as it otherwise might be perceived.

Lean but Agile Optimizes Work

We offer a look at the traditional approach to business planning compared to the Lean but Agile approach, which optimizes the workforce to achieve the organization's objectives.

The Traditional Approach

Traditionally, business plans and forecasts are developed in one of several ways. One common approach is to focus business strategy primarily—and emphatically—on finance and marketing with less attention devoted to production (in manufacturing), operations (in service firms), and human resources. Sales forecasts are developed based on estimates of how much people will buy from the company, given past experiences with sales and with the state of the general business cycle (economic conditions), or what services are needed from a business. Products and services have a *product* or *service life cycle* in which sales improve to a certain point and then plateau unless new enhancements are made or products/services are created. Of course, sales are also affected by the general economy, with people less willing to purchase discretionary goods in tough economic times. Each sale translates into a share of money for meeting the company or business's overhead expenses (such as employees) and profits after expenses.

With this traditional approach, human resources are usually considered at the end of the planning process. It is typically assumed that a given number of people will be required to make a certain number of products or deliver a given amount of service. This gives rise to the longstanding traditional view of economists, who speak about "demand for labor" and "supply of labor." *Demand* simply means "how many people we will need to make a forecasted number of products or deliver a forecasted level of service." In contrast, *supply* means "how many people we have now to meet the demand."

In the traditional approach, little attention is devoted to actual differences in productivity among individuals or to how important some worker groups are to achieving an organization's unique competitive advantage, sometimes called *core competency* (what it does better than competitors). For planning, it is generally assumed that "x" number of people will yield "y" amount of products or services. If product or service demand declines, the workforce will thus need to be reduced through downsizing or some other method (such as "early out" offers or even short-term furloughs). If product or service demand increases, the workforce must be increased to match expected production or service requirements.

In the traditional approach, decision makers usually begin their planning by making the assumption that the current organization's staffing pattern will remain largely unchanged. Poor performers are not necessarily "let go"; outstanding performers are not necessarily rewarded in line with measurable results. Despite much talk to the contrary, seniority continues to play a major role in managing staff. Managers also find it exceptionally difficult to rid themselves of poor performers due to progressive disciplinary policies, union grievance procedures, industrial agreements, and concerns over violating discrimination laws.

The Lean but Agile Work Approach

The Lean but Agile work approach differs from the traditional approach in that it takes the long view by systemically planning the work and the workforce to achieve results. However, leadership commitment to the Lean but Agile strategy is critical. To garner this kind of support requires the creation of a business plan and attention to the return on investment (ROI). (We deal with this and the process of implementing a Lean but Agile program in chapter 7.) Once leadership support is secured, Lean but Agile work focuses initially on the business plan. The length of the plan is less important than determining what the business will look like upon full implementation.

By focusing initial attention on the work, decision makers can crystallize where the organization is headed and clarify what it will look like when success is achieved. As in our analogy, there is a need to determine initially if the objective—in this case the end stage—is actually achievable. The business plan is used as the initial foundation for determining potential achievement. If no business plan exists, then decision makers should follow the steps for creating one described in chapter 7.

Example 2-4: A Consulting Engagement

A recent consulting engagement required one author to assess a service organization's understanding of workforce planning and review the current situation in the organization. It did not surprise the consultant to discover that terminology varied. Some thought that criticality related to any position not filled. Some thought any role open for more than (n) weeks was automatically critical. Others defined a gap in any management position as critical. No standard understanding of criticality existed. The result: confused priorities for all HR activities.

This situation dramatizes that decision makers who follow a traditional approach to workforce planning often find themselves devolving into crisis management. All HR efforts focus on closing immediate gaps in hiring, training, and retraining. Stakeholders make decisions based on immediate needs without considering future requirements that would be achieved through a Lean but Agile program. Work activity and hiring decisions are made without the required assessment of future needs, for example, without considering:

- What work was really required to be delivered by the organization directly?
- Were permanent staff members really required?
- Would contractors be more efficient, effective, and economical?
- Would outsourced services provide a better output?

A more in-depth review of ways work can be done is found in chapter 4.

Review Organizational Strategic Objectives and the Business Plan

The lean work process component of a Lean but Agile program may be as simple as reviewing an existing business plan or creating one. The following model depicts the flow of the overall Lean but Agile workforce program:

DEFINITION—TRANSITION—ACTION

1. Turn business plans into strategies.
2. Turn strategies into outcomes.
3. Define what the outcomes look like.
4. Compare it to today.
5. Determine what works and what does not.
6. Find out why it is broken.
7. Find out how we fix it.
8. Find out for whom, by whom, and with what.
9. Implement audit, review, and feedback.

All the steps above are achieved through clearly defined ownership and objectives.

While "Definition, Transition, and Action" outline the life cycle of a typical Lean but Agile program, the focus of this chapter is to define the "zero base future state." A *zero base future state* assumes that a new organization will be created at a projected date. It emphasizes describing the "future state" organizational objective(s) and what the organization will look like in structure, capability, and delivery when it has successfully delivered that *objective*.

Of course, the current and forecasted business activity will impact decisions about future positions. But in this initial step we should concentrate on the most efficient, effective, and economical delivery of those future organizational goals and then determine the most appropriate mechanism(s) to deliver them.

1. Turn Business Plans into Strategies
Review the Plan: Understanding Organizational Strategic Objectives

Many organizations work with a short-term focus. Some work on much longer cycles, ten to twenty years, while others consider eighteen months a long time. The key focus is the forecasted situation at whatever that designated point may be. The plan is then analyzed and discussed. At this stage the vision and mission are accepted as is, unless, of course, a plan does not exist. The plan may need to be revisited once the analysis is completed. Consider the following questions:

- What is the core objective of the organization at that future point?
- What key goals support this core objective?
  1. Where is the evidence that this objective and these goals can be achieved?
  2. What will the organization look like (structure, service lines, and so forth) at that point, "a zero base future state"?

It is important to assess whether the targets are realistic. Aspirational goals not based on data or facts are and will continue to be used by some decision makers as the foundation for objectives. Vigilance is needed, however, in managing service delivery expectations. Failing to achieve goals can have an impact on the workforce.

When this review step is finished, leaders should have a detailed understanding of the organizational strategic objectives and key deliverables. They will have assessed the likelihood of achieving success and made any adjustments to the objectives or timelines to bring them in line with the current situation. For example, as with many business plan reviews, the *objectives* may need to be realigned as it may not be possible with the current organizational structure or focus to deliver them in the time frame required.

2. Turn Strategies into Outcomes

Review the Design of the Future State

Next it is essential to devise an understanding of what the organization will look like functionally at the designated point in time. What key functions are needed to deliver the outcomes, goals, and objectives? A *function* is an activity that produces *outputs*. A function may be the equivalent activity of a whole department or only part of one. For example, manufacturing can be a function, or it may be broken down further into production as one function and prototype design as another. The decision is based on the organization's industry, targeted outcomes, and activities. This is in line with the Katz and Kahn's views of subsystems.[6]

The process to achieve this, as described in the "Review Organizational Strategic Objectives and the Business Plan" section above, requires a facilitated discussion with senior leaders and reviews the proposed organizational structure either as described in the business plan or as created through the process with reference to the organization's current position.

A note of caution: Too often, functions are hailed as the core of the organization and the key to success, when in reality the function is uncompetitive and is not delivering economical, effective, or efficient *outputs*.

Example 2-5: Firm X

An engineering firm (Firm X) contracted one author of this volume to assist with a review of the firm's business plan for three years to make the case to expand its manufacturing capability. While Firm X was a small enterprise, the engagement encapsulated the ideas of Lean but Agile work. At the time of the consulting engagement, Firm X had been in the manufacturing sector for more than thirty years. It had generated more than $100 million in sales of heavy equipment components and had an excellent reputation for quality design and delivery. Firm X had seen solid growth for twenty-six of those years. But the firm was facing growing competition as competitors were increasingly winning bids and tenders. The new CEO was given a directive by the board to turn the situation around.

The managers of Firm X had never considered that the firm would be anything other than a manufacturer. Its five-year plan was focused on return on investment and reduction of debt.

An initial environmental scan, analysis of the competition, and a review of the firm's strategy quickly revealed that Firm X could not deliver value for money from the manufacturing function, even with a proposed multimillion-dollar investment in new equipment.

This engagement was initially focused on preparing a business case for further expansion. Once the environmental scan was completed, the evidence supported a much deeper intervention.

In reviewing the firm's business plan it became apparent that the leaders were so focused on maintaining the status quo that they had simply ignored the objectives of the longer-term plan. The business plan had quite specific (and achievable) objectives and deliverables. But it had been ignored for the better part of eighteen months because the focus was on winning the next bid.

When the data gathering, evidence, and analysis of the business position were completed in this review and the business plan was revised, decision makers agreed that the organization needed to review all functions based on a simple value for money proposition if it was to meet its objectives. As defined in our terminology, the questions were related to the economy, the efficiency, and the effectiveness of delivering each function.

A plan was designed to be delivered over three years with predominantly the same workforce. Significant milestones were established along the way to ensure that the whole organization was focused on Firm X's objectives. Extensive change management programs and communications plans were implemented with an emphasis on clear, precise communication. A change management strategy similar to Kotter's 8-Step Change Management Model was used, and an emphasis on the building of trust across all levels of the organization was paramount.[7]

The end result was that Firm X outsourced manufacturing, concentrating internal effort on design and prototype construction using a flexible labor pool as required. The business sublet its stores and distribution services.

The author continued to be engaged by Firm X throughout the plan's implementation. Although there were several difficult times throughout the process, this firm increased its business significantly. Its former competitors realized that Firm X was a superior design and prototype fabrication facility. The outsourcing of manufacturing and the subletting of its stores and distribution all yielded additional profit.

Throughout the planned transition the firm's workforce was significantly reshaped, reeducated, and refocused. The focus was firmly fixed on *outcomes*, not *outputs* or *processes*.

3. Define What the Outcomes Look Like

Define Functions and Functional Criticality

Once the organizational structure is established, the leaders should look at each function by considering two questions:

1. What functions are critical to deliver the targeted objective?
2. What functions provide value for money?

Functions: As defined previously, a function may be the equivalent activity of a whole department or a subset of a department. For example, in the initial review of Firm X in Example 2-5, manufacturing was regarded as the major function. With analysis, this was broken into two functions—prototype design, and manufacture and volume production.

Value for money: These indicators are used to assess the "value for money" of an activity:

1. *Efficiency:* The use of resources so that output is optimized for any given set of resource inputs, or input is minimized for any given quantity or quality of output.
2. *Effectiveness:* The achievement of the objectives or other intended effects of activities at a program or entity level.
3. *Economy:* The acquisition of the appropriate quality and quantity of resources at the appropriate times and at the lowest cost. Figure 2-3 illustrates the three E's.

Figure 2-3: The Three E's

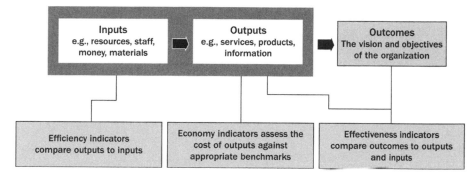

It is also important to conduct an evidence-based assessment for each of the three E's. For instance, the initial meetings with the leaders of Firm X indicated their strong belief that the problem with manufacturing was simply outdated machinery. The root cause, when finally evidenced, included the diminished flexibility and capacity of the facility, uncompetitive processes, and inflexible labor provisions and labor costs. When evidence that new equipment would result in a turnaround in profitability for Firm X was asked for, none could be found. As the facts came to light, the leaders were shocked. In this instance the evidence, gathered through the initial consulting activity, took the shape of a financial analysis, a market analysis, and client interviews.

The answers to the questions on function and value for money are best acquired through a facilitated discussion.

The output from this component of defining functions and functional criticality is a description of an organizational framework that is best suited to deliver the organizational strategic objectives at a future point.

Understanding Criticality

The authors' experience indicates that a significant lack of understanding exists about how the term *critical* should be applied to function and competency or, in some instances, if there is a need to assess criticality in the first place. To some managers, any vacancy is critical. To others, criticality is determined by the organizational chart, where only management positions are critical.

There are many models for determining the criticality of a role or position. The public sector has done significant work on the development of a matrix-style analysis. Also, many leading human resources commentators offer versions of criticality, including John Sullivan in his paper "Leveraging a Position Prioritization Methodology to Deliver Truly Strategic HR."[8]

A simple matrix of criticality is shown in Figure 2-4.

Figure 2-4: Review the Work and Workforce to Plan for the Future

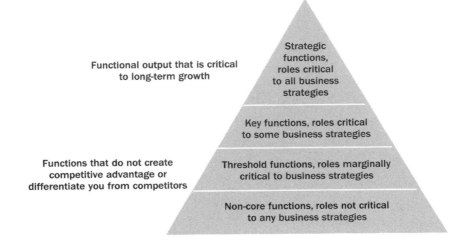

Defining and focusing on organizational goals as related to HCM

Functional output that is critical to long-term growth

Strategic functions, roles critical to all business strategies

Key functions, roles critical to some business strategies

Functions that do not create competitive advantage or differentiate you from competitors

Threshold functions, roles marginally critical to business strategies

Non-core functions, roles not critical to any business strategies

Critical Functions

Once an understanding of what the organization wants to achieve by the designated time is reviewed and either confirmed or reestablished, and there is an outline of what leaders believe the organization should look like, the *outcomes* should be revisited to confirm their appropriateness and that timing aligns with the latest understanding of the objective.

A matrix can then be created with the "x" axis listing the *outcomes* of the organization and the "y" axis describing the functions within this future state model, for example, manufacturing, distribution, sales, research and development, finance and administration, human resources, and information technology. A review of each of the *outcomes* then asks, "What is critical to the successful delivery of this outcome?" (typically, the top ten to twelve points). Additionally, what evidence exists that this is the case?

Critical Roles

Critical roles are those currently crucial to the achievement of the organizational outcomes. They significantly influence the organization's ability to achieve its objectives. The impact timeline should be measured in days, possibly weeks, but never months. Critical roles will change as the demand for expertise changes over time. A vacancy in a critical role will have a significantly tangible impact on the organization's ability to deliver outputs, achieve goals, or meet budget requirements.

Identify Types of Critical Roles in the Organization

There are many pathways to identifying an organization's critical roles. But whichever model is chosen as most suitable, it is imperative that the model be understood by all the staff members involved in workforce planning or management

Look Back from This Future State to Today

Once the objectives, goals, and structure of the organization's future state have been established, the leaders must plot a course from the current situation. Much like the second group of climbers in the earlier analogy, staff members must anticipate potential issues and milestones along the way toward making the ultimate objective a reality. In Example 2-5, Firm X needed to transition from a struggling manufacturer to a successful design and prototype fabrication facility. The firm did so by outsourcing functions. This was a significant change in the firm's function that did not occur overnight. A plan based on the firm's future state was developed over a period of three years. With a sound business plan, the organization set key milestones to be achieved along the way, including adopting an outsourced manufacturing model and creating an internal talent pool to prepare apprentices and junior engineers.

This plan thus formed the blueprint for the firm's work requirements. The creation of the plan followed the standard business planning model adopted by the organization. Firm X concentrated on ensuring that the linkages between outputs and outcomes were continually reviewed, particularly at important milestones.

Map Critical Work Within the Functions

Once a framework for the functional requirements of the organization is established, the next step is to analyze positions or roles critical to each function. Again the question driving this process is this: *How do these positions contribute to the overall outcome?* If the focus is constantly on the outcome(s), the model develops quite quickly.

The mapping of these positions begins with examining the desired future position and working back to the current situation. This way each milestone of the organization's objective will be informed by the needs of the next milestone.

Identify Competency Requirements for Functions/Work

Once we have identified the work that requires staffing, we must clearly understand the required skills demanded by the work before sourcing people to do that work. Understanding the required skill sets sounds basic. But the fact is that most organizations do not have an accurate view of the competency requirements needed by staff members to perform their work—and particularly to perform it very well. It follows that if you do not have a clear idea of what is needed, finding it is very challenging!

Finding the right people could start by identifying the profession needed. But doing that rarely provides sufficiently precise information. For example, you may need a chef. Clearly, the skill sets of a chef vary widely, and one who is proficient at preparing Korean dishes may have no ability to make Greek food. The same principle applies to software developers, accountants, engineers, and most other professions. The *specific* work requires individuals best suited for that work.

Many organizations have developed job descriptions to assist with the identification of these job specifications. If your organization has them, they can provide some useful information for matching workers with the job. And yet the job descriptions found in most organizations today are only minimally useful for implementing Lean but Agile work. Here are some of their limitations:

■ Their strongest point is that they are typically a fairly comprehensive list of job responsibilities, even though today, for a variety of reasons such as rapid change and lean staffing, these are not typically and systematically maintained by most organizations.

■ Job descriptions often do include other information that has the potential to help us match work and workers, such as the required education and experience, working conditions, compensable factors, amount of supervision or autonomy, and even required knowledge, skills, and abilities (KSAs), but the processes used to gather these data are rarely adequate to produce accurate information. In chapter 3 we look at how these and other elements can be more effectively used than they are now to help better match work with workers.

■ Even when a job description lists accurate and current job responsibilities, it does not provide corresponding information about what responsibilities can be completed by the available pool of workers. Hence, individuals cannot be easily matched to those job descriptions. This problem is greatly compounded because there is typically little or no overlap between the ways job responsibilities are stated on different job descriptions, even when the jobs are closely related. Therefore, in a medium or large organization with hundreds of job descriptions, it would be necessary to assess workers for potentially hundreds or even thousands of job responsibilities, an obvious impracticality.

■ Job descriptions are designed with the assumption that individuals will acquit all the responsibilities given. But I can but Agile is not well-served by traditional notions of static, unchanging jobs that must be completed in their entirety by individuals. Rather, the goal is to pick optimal responsibilities for individuals based on both their capabilities and current organizational needs. Therefore, an individual's responsibilities should be viewed as fluid rather than static.

■ The methodology used to develop most job descriptions is not optimal for identifying which individuals can most successfully complete the work. Traditionally, analysts look at the job responsibilities and try to tease out what KSAs might be required. The first problem with this is that it is difficult to look at job responsibilities and accurately identify important KSAs. Second, KSAs do not go far enough as they do not identify behaviors and values that characterize highly successful performers. These behaviors and values are not just "nice to have." They can often spell the difference between successful and unsuccessful performance. For example, a banker may know everything about mortgages but lack integrity. A basketball player may have excellent passing skills but never use them because he is not a team player.

The most effective software developer is not always the one who is the most technically proficient. We have seen examples of *less* technical programmers who are masterful in their time management and at looking at an existing code and quickly homing in on likely problem areas that might be causing a defect, instead of overanalyzing exactly how every line of code works.

■   Traditionally, KSAs have, over time—as many observations and studies of top performers have shown—indicated that certain traits and values and the resultant behaviors are also critical. Knowledge and skills are not enough. Competence *does begin* with having the required knowledge and skills to perform the job; piloting skills are needed to safely land a jumbo jet, and no airline would knowingly hire a pilot who lacked the requisite skills to do so. But knowledge and skills are not enough. Anything that leads to job success—such as personality characteristics, achievement motivation, awareness of bodies of knowledge—is included in competence. In one instance in 2009, the pilots of a Northwest Airlines flight missed their destination airport by 150 miles because they reportedly were engaged in a heated discussion over airline policy.[9] They knew what to do, but for reasons other than lack of knowledge and skill ended up not performing adequately.

The Role of Competencies in Understanding Work and Integrating Talent Management

To help address the challenges that job descriptions create for optimally matching work and people, many organizations worldwide now analyze the job competencies (often just called *competencies*) that are required to get work done. We define competence (or a competent worker) as someone who is *able* to perform a given assignment "to standard" or "consistent with expectations." Depending on the work to be done, we might require novice, advanced, or expert competence. Not surprisingly, competence requires competencies. The term *competency* can be (pragmatically) defined as any characteristic of an individual performer that leads to effective or outstanding performance. While no universal agreement exists on what individual characteristics qualify as competencies, we believe that successful individual performance requires a combination of job knowledge, skills, traits (or abilities), and values. Each competency is further defined by behaviors (sometimes called *behavioral indicators*). Most often, positive behaviors are defined, but some organizations also like to define negative behaviors that should be detected and minimized.

Competencies are often classified into different types. *Core competencies* are those required of every employee in the organization. *Cross-functional competencies* are those that are important in many different types of jobs, such as planning, communication, or budgeting. *Technical* (or *functional*) competencies are related to a worker's primary duties, such as tax accounting, C++ software programming, or employee training. *Threshold* competencies are those that are needed to "play the game." For example, a pilot needs to know how to land an airplane. *Differentiating* competencies distinguish superior from average performers.

Since many descriptions of competencies can be vague and subjective (for example, "teamwork"), typically *behavioral indicators* are developed. Behaviors can be observed and provide a forecast for how people can be successful in a particular job. Figure 2-5 shows how behavioral indicators can help more clearly define competencies.

Figure 2-5: Example 1: Customer Focus Competency and Related Behavioral Indicators

Customer focus description: Seeks to discover and meet the needs of external and internal *customers*

Behavioral Indicators:
1. Asks questions to identify customer's needs
2. Develops partnerships with customers, acts as trusted advisor
3. Looks for creative approaches to provide or improve service to customers
4. Takes prompt action to resolve customer problems or concerns

In virtually every job, some people perform the work better than others. As a rule of thumb, organizational psychologists have demonstrated that on average a performer at the 80th percentile is about twice as productive as someone at the 20th percentile. Top performers do the important things more consistently, especially under challenging circumstances, and they also do different things. Unlike most job descriptions that list KSAs based on looking at the job tasks, competencies are determined by looking at people, typically highly effective performers. Looking at effective performers provides different, more complete information than looking just at job tasks. To use an athlete as an example, what competencies did Michael Jordan, considered by many to be the best basketball player of all time, bring to the sport? Although he had exceptional physical skills (he was referred to as "Air Jordan" because of his great leaping skills), he was also well-known for his desire to win, intensity, concentration, and attitude. The most successful athlete will not necessarily be the one who is the strongest, runs the fastest, or jumps the highest. But values and/or traits such as teamwork, tenacity, motivation and dedication, and character can spell the difference between good and great performance.

The use of competencies has other benefits besides being one of the best ways to match work and people:

- They provide a clearer path to high performance because they identify behaviors that can guide individual performers, coaches, and feedback or evaluations.

- They stay current longer than lists of job responsibilities.

- Competencies may be easier to link to organizational strategy because they can be tied more easily to organizational capabilities that are the source of its competitive advantage. For example, if innovation is central to an organization's strategy, individuals may be encouraged to demonstrate creativity and even calculated risk taking to support this strategy.

Competencies are becoming central to employee development, performance management, succession and workforce planning, and in general to having the right people in place at the right time and at the right cost. Further, competencies are very useful for unifying human resources functions that traditionally have been separate and managed independently of each other, such as recruiting, selection, and compensation, which could be much more effective if they were used in unison. This approach is often referred to as *integrated talent management,* and the goals are typically loftier than traditional HR metrics. We define *Integrated Talent Management* (ITM) as a plan to increase the capabilities and productivity of the workforce over time through coordinated talent-management approaches, tools, and resources in response to the changing needs of a business, a dynamic economy, and a changing talent market. Figure 2-6 depicts integrated talent management. Note that competency management appears in the middle of that model.

There have been many research studies that lend credence to the view that the use of competencies and integrated talent management makes a difference. Watson Wyatt studied 168 high-performing companies with excel-

Figure 2-6: The Vision of Integrated Talent Management

Source: Bersin & Associates, 2008.

lent financial performance for three years.[10] The companies were selected from a range of sectors, including manufacturing, high-tech, healthcare, energy, finance, and service organizations. The study found that defining job competencies was one of the top three initiatives key to future success. The Aberdeen Group found that when organizations can define required competencies, assess the use of them, and use them throughout the talent-management cycle, it promotes impressive business results, such as significantly higher profit per employee, customer satisfaction, and customer retention.[11] Bersin Associates research shows that organizations with superior, integrated talent management show 26 percent higher revenue per employee, 40 percent lower turnover among employees, 87 percent greater ability to hire the best people, and 92 percent greater ability to respond to changing economic conditions.[12] A Watson Wyatt competency study found that companies that take an integrated talent-management approach are better at attracting and retaining high performers and more likely to be high-performing organizations.[13]

Competency Models: Bridges Between Work and People Requirements

A *competency model* is a set of the most critical competencies employed by highly successful performers to complete their work. Therefore, competency models are extremely useful for selecting and assigning workers, for individual development, for evaluating bench strength and succession planning, and for future workforce planning.

A *job* (for example, customer service representative) competency model identifies the ten to thirty competencies required to successfully complete the six to fifteen responsibilities typically identified in a job description. A *role* competency model focuses on only one responsibility or outcome, or sometimes two or three closely related responsibilities, and therefore the model may include three to six competencies.

Most often, competencies are identified by a trained competency modeling facilitator and a small group of knowledgeable persons called subject matter experts (SMEs), who understand how successful performers do their work. SMEs are typically either highly effective performers or supervisors who have had the opportunity to observe the approaches of highly effective performers. Instead of theorizing about what competencies might be important, the group focuses as much as possible on the competencies they know to be important from their experience. This approach is more likely to result in accurate, comprehensive models.

Because competency models are based on job responsibilities (or sometimes required outputs or outcomes), these models are best created as part of a systematic job analysis or *job profiling* designed specifically to provide a competency model. Rather than beginning with competency identification, it is important to first identify or verify the critical responsibilities and their priority. After the competencies are chosen, it is advisable to link each to one or more responsibilities. Showing that a competency is job- or role-related provides both a legal foundation for defending decisions made based on the competency model and insight into the ranking of the importance of competencies. It usually makes practical sense, given that SMEs have been assembled to update an existing job description while creating a competency model. In sum, competency models should not be created in isolation; rather, they should typically be created as part of a structured process. This systematic process is what we call *job profiling*.

Figure 2-7: Steps in Job-Profiling Process

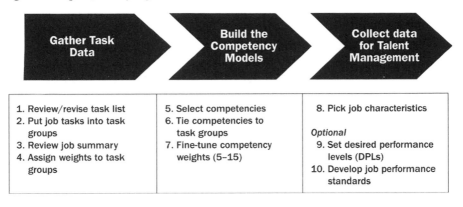

Gather Task Data	Build the Competency Models	Collect data for Talent Management
1. Review/revise task list 2. Put job tasks into task groups 3. Review job summary 4. Assign weights to task groups	5. Select competencies 6. Tie competencies to task groups 7. Fine-tune competency weights (5–15)	8. Pick job characteristics *Optional* 9. Set desired performance levels (DPLs) 10. Develop job performance standards

Figure 2-7 shows the steps in a job profiling process we have developed that we and others have used successfully to model thousands of jobs.

Other Important Elements of Work That Need to Be Defined and Understood

Defining required competencies is one of the most important enhancements to work analysis, but we do not mean to ignore the value of defining work by performance standards, education requirements and certifications, required experience, and work characteristics (for example, compensation, reporting relationship, type of supervision, amount of structure, interaction with others, travel, working conditions). These are all discussed further in chapter 3, where we look at creating a talent pool and how to select individuals who are a good fit for work assignments. The bottom line is that any element of work that is known to impact worker recruitment, engagement, success, and retention is relevant to Lean but Agile workforces because it will in turn impact worker output, availability, and cost, the three key pillars of an optimized workforce.

Chapter Summary

This chapter investigated the need to focus on organizational strategic objectives and to understand what work must be completed at an organizational and functional level. It discussed the importance of determining criticality; Outcome-Based Management (OM); and the framework of input, process, output, and outcome that supports it. OM is a strategic approach to ensure that initiatives are designed around planned outcomes. The Outcome Management Framework (OMF) is a planning and management approach to guide the formulation of outcomes to achieve the desired organizational strategic objectives. OMF is focused on *why things are done*. The focus of the latter is on *purpose* rather than on just *process* or *process improvement* alone.

This chapter reviewed the following model of the Lean but Agile workforce program:

- Turn business plans into strategies.
- Turn strategies into outcomes.
- Define what the outcomes look like.
- Compare it to today.
- Determine what works and what does not.
- Find out why it is broken.
- Find out how we fix it.
- Find out for whom, by whom, and with what.
- Implement audit, review, and feedback.

3

CREATE A TALENT POOL FOR A LEAN BUT AGILE WORKFORCE

A LEAN WORKFORCE is achieved by selecting people from your organization talent pool and assigning them to the right work at the right time and the right costs. By *workforce*, we mean all the individuals who *are currently* working on assignments for your organization. By *organization talent pool*, we mean all the individuals whom you have recruited and prequalified to complete work assignments for today or the future whether they are part of the current workforce or not. Full-time employees are members of the current workforce and the talent pool. Part-time workers, contractors, consultants, interns, and others are also usually part of the mix; some of them may be part of the workforce today, and all are part of the organization talent pool. Some prefer to speak of the *talent inventory* instead of the *talent pool*, but the term *inventory* can evoke the image of an interchangeable commodity. Therefore, we prefer the term *pool*.

Chances are you already know a lot about the members of your workforce, particularly the full-time employees. You know their skill sets, their cost, and their availability to do your organization's work. You probably know their past experience, strengths, and areas of needed development. You may even know their work preferences and career aspirations. Your workforce is filled with individuals with *known* capabilities, but generally much less is known about other persons who are well qualified to play a valuable role in your organization. When forced to go outside the workforce to search for people, most organizations are faced with longer search times, higher recruiting expenses, potentially higher compensation costs, greater uncertainty about the quality of people selected, and the possibility that the talent you need is not available when you need it. By contrast, if you construct a talent pool and get to know its members as thoroughly as your current workforce, you won't face the drawbacks typically associated with searching outside your organization. Getting to know *in advance* those who are in a position to help you is key to using a talent pool and creating a lean workforce.

Whereas *lean* is desirable for workforces, ideally talent pools are *ample* so that they will provide you with alternatives for getting the work done. When you have staffing *options*, you are more likely to achieve a lean workforce. A *mature talent pool* is one that comes close to providing "one-stop shopping," that is, a place where most talent needs can be satisfied. Even with a mature organization talent pool, there will probably be times when you will need to go to the public talent pool (made up of all working individuals), but the potential of those workers to assist is mainly unknown.

An *optimized workforce* (those persons working for you today) and an *optimized talent pool* (those individuals potentially working for you tomorrow) are defined similarly. By *optimized* we mean a workforce or talent pool that provides the organization with individuals who, to the greatest extent possible, (1) consistently achieve desired results, (2) are available when needed, and (3) are maximally cost-effective. Optimizing is a process for effectively matching work with workforces and is foundational for achieving a Lean but Agile workforce. Keep in mind, especially if you utilize full-time employees, that optimizing also requires that you regularly optimize the *assignments* of your workers.

Globalization, technology, and the nature of work in the information age have increased competition and lowered pricing for many products and services, but at the same time they have also created unprecedented opportunities for leveraging workforce optimization into a competitive advantage. Despite having so much to gain, many organizations conduct business with little knowledge of workforce talent and no organization talent pool. Under these circumstances, the workforce will always be suboptimized. The closest most organizations come today to creating a talent pool is the creation of succession-planning replacement charts and/or pools, most typically just for senior leadership positions.

The steps to creating a lean workforce are (1) build a mature talent pool (the focus of this chapter), (2) optimize the mix of full-time employees and alternative workers, and (3) modify talent-management and work-scheduling practices (see chapter 6 for our discussion of items 2 and 3). Creating a lean workforce is a "young science," and we can expect to see improvements in all three steps of the process in the near future. Value can be gained by implementing any one of them, and even more so by doing all three. Identifying strategic, high-impact work (in chapter 2) and considering the full range of alternative workers (in chapter 4) are also important.

Identify Workers Who Consistently Achieve Desired Results

Most if not all organizations desire talent that *consistently achieves desired results*. The challenge is identifying a talent selection approach that is valid (accurate), reliable (consistent), practical (affordable in terms of time and cost), and legally defensible. Keep in mind that you need to thoroughly understand the talent in your workforce *and* your organization talent pool. Ideally, we recommend that you evaluate talent based on five indicators: (1) performance history; (2) competence; (3) education, including certifications; (4) experience, including critical qualifications; and (5) personal preferences, including job characteristic preferences. Although this is not as simple as just looking at data from annual performance reviews, the good news is that the approaches and tools needed to collect these data are generally familiar as well as within the reach of most organizations. Further, although it is best to have all of this information, having some data is usually better than having none, and each organization can tweak talent assessment after considering the tradeoffs of the value of the talent indicators versus the costs of collection. For those who lack either the expertise, time, or desire to collect the needed information, outside resources are usually available to assist.

Performance History: The First Indicator of Talent

We agree with the often-stated maxim that *the best single predictor of future performance is past performance.* The power of past performance to predict future performance is even greater when we have multiple data points that allow us to see consistent trends over time. More recent reviews will typically be better predictors of future performance and can be given a little heavier weight than earlier reviews. Also, when past performance reviews reflect assignments similar to potential new assignments, they will be stronger evidence of what can be expected next from an individual.

Most organizations already evaluate individual performance one or several times each year through programs variously called performance management, performance planning and review, or performance appraisal. The more effective programs require a role-specific, individual performance plan for each individual (see Figure 3-1). The goals, standards, and/or competencies in the plan also lay out a performance review tailored to the responsibilities of the individual.

The track record of most performance appraisal programs has been mixed at best, and many organizations perfunctorily "go through the motions" because of a perceived lack of value. The direction provided by a solid performance planning and review process, however, is more important in a lean organization than in a traditional organization for several reasons. The clear direction and tacit knowledge included in a properly developed performance plan provide the critical direction needed when work roles are fluid and more people perform the work, as is likely to be the case for an organization that regularly optimizes the assignments of its talent. Performance plans help ensure that the organization receives predictable, consistent performance regardless of who performs the work. Larger spans of control in lean, flatter organizations also argue for the clarity provided by a performance plan. Performance reviews are also more important because they are likely to be used more frequently in a lean organization to determine job assignments.

The process of workforce optimization whereby organizations frequently review and optimize work assignments of talent provides a real opportunity to improve both the validity and reliability of performance reviews. Although an *annual* performance plan and review has been standard,

Figure 3-1: Sample Performance Plan

Individual Goals ⊕Add

Goal #1
Analyze retention issues

✎Edit Goal ↻Assign ♡Delete Goal

Linked to Goal: 🔍Expense Management - Supervisor's Individual Goal

Assigned By: AUB Administrator
Status: ✎In Progress - On Track
Appraisal Weight: ✎20%

Created on: Tue, Jan 6, 2004
Planned Start Date: Sat, Mar 1, 2008
Planned Completion Date: Sat, Nov 8, 2008
Revised Completion Date: Wed, Nov 18, 2009

Standards ✎Edit

Standard #1
Completes tasks in a timely manner

♡Delete Standard

Appraisal Weight: ✎15%

Task Group: 🔍HR Direction

Notes: (0) ⊕Add Note

Competencies ✎Edit

Competency #1
Customer Focused

♡Delete Competency

Appraisal Weight: ✎10%

Description:
Listens to internal and external customers and assigns the highest priority to their satisfaction. Inspires a passion for excellence and quality in every aspect of work. the organization.

Notes: (0) ⊕Add Note

workforce optimization benefits from an *assignment*-based approach, that is, a performance plan and one or more reviews for each significant assignment. This does not mean that the performance plan and review need to be developed "from scratch" each time someone is assigned, be it the last person to perform the role or someone new. Rather, each plan should ideally build on the plan that was developed when the work was most recently performed. An assignment-based performance plan can include the same elements as any good annual performance plan (that is, goals, standards, and competencies).

The performance plan is like a road map. It defines where the worker is going. It should also provide tips and insight on the best route to follow, dictating (when needed) action steps, required support, and behaviors or practices used by persons who are successful with this assignment. Identifying the competencies required for the assignment expedites the process of determining who within the talent pool can do it well and at an acceptable cost. Here are some of the potential advantages of an assignment-based performance review:

- It is simpler to set and gain agreement on clear goals and/or performance standards for an assignment than it is to anticipate and create an annual plan.
- Assignment-based goals are more likely to accurately and completely describe the work that an individual is doing, which enhances both the understanding of what is required and the review process.
- Presuming that many assignments are repeated, the quality of the performance plan (goals and best practices) can be systematically fine-tuned while the work to create future performance plans is minimized. Once developed for an assignment, the plan is available for reuse or reference; it is not necessary to re-create the goals or the evaluation each time an assignment is done.
- Assignments are often well-suited to multirater feedback from either internal/external customers or team members. Multirater feedback typically provides more valid information than a review by a single reviewer.

Good performance plans (and therefore the performance reviews) can be efficiently developed using subject matter experts, usually workers and supervisors with a track record of success with the assignment, and a trained facilitator. Good performance plans will pay dividends far beyond the benefits achieved by most performance review systems today.

Worker Competence: The Second Indicator of Talent

Increasingly, organizations are beginning to implement a second type of individual evaluation called a *competency assessment* (or development assessment). As noted in chapter 2, we defined a competent worker as someone who can perform a given assignment "to standard" or "consistent with expectations." Depending on the assignment, a beginning or advanced level of competency may be required. We define competencies fairly broadly, as either knowledge (for example, policies or laws applicable to one's work), skills (for example, welding, C++ programming), traits (for example, tenacity, detail orientation), or values (for example, integrity, customer focus) that are needed to perform a task well. Competencies can also be divided into *core competencies* (required for all in the organization), *cross-functional competencies* (for example, time management, budgeting) that apply broadly to many types of work, and *technical competencies* such as heavy water chemistry or building security.

Competencies are demonstrated through behaviors (sometimes called behavioral indicators), which are defined in advance so that we have a clear idea of what is meant by the competency, which in turn helps workers to understand expectations and helps evaluators to make valid and fair assessments of competence. Most assignments or jobs require multiple competencies. Depending on circumstances, three to six competencies might be identified for an assignment, and fifteen to thirty might be identified for an entire job, since jobs typically include several assignments.

Some may argue that performance history is sufficient; that a separate competency assessment isn't needed. According to this line of thought, if someone performs to expectations, it really doesn't matter how we evaluate her competence, and if she doesn't perform to expectations, particularly after being told that she needs to improve, she should be reassigned to more appropriate work or terminated.

Our point of view is that competency assessments are required information for optimizing workforces and talent pools and for providing many other benefits. Recent studies (several were cited in chapter 2, including those by Watson Wyatt, Aberdeen, and Bersin Associates) document the benefits of competency identification and assessment. To reiterate, the benefits include greater ability to hire the best people, lower turnover among high performers, greater ability to respond to changing conditions, as well as outcomes such as higher profit per worker and better customer satisfaction and retention.

Whereas performance reviews are generally very useful for telling us *what* happened, competency assessments are often superior for providing insight into *why*. Certainly competency assessments provide uniquely important information on employee development to help good performers do even better and subpar performers to meet expectations. Further, competency assessments are a more versatile tool than performance reviews for identifying the right individual for a *new* assignment or assigning an individual to work where he or she can provide the most value. Work over time evolves and job assignments will change. However, many of the underlying competencies required to complete the work may remain consistent. Even when totally new competencies are required, it is simpler to match individual competencies with the competency profile of the assignment than to match previous performance reviews with the current job description. Competencies are likely to maintain this advantage at least until the day that an organization develops a standard taxonomy of job tasks that is used consistently in each job description or role description.

Beyond the benefits of making optimal job assignments or populating the organization talent pool, competency assessments provide information that helps break down HR silos and create an integrated talent-management approach; competencies and competency models can be used for the entire life cycle of a worker. Specifically, a single competency model can be used for recruitment and selection, training, career development, succession and workforce planning, and even transition out of the organization. Rather than having recruitment use one set of criteria for hiring, onboarding a second set, training a third, succession planning still something else, etc., the same competency models and assessments can be used for all of these. Naturally, having all of these formerly disparate systems driving in the same direction provides better results as well as labor and cost savings in developing these different but related functional areas of human resources.

Use Simple Ratings to Measure Worker Competence

Most often today, competency assessments are done by using what we will call a *simple rating*. Figure 3-2 shows an example of such a rating for the competency "strategic planning and focus." A simple competency rating instrument typically includes somewhere in the range of ten to thirty competencies that are taken from a relevant competency model. Frequently, a generic competency model is used, for example, a supervisor assessment that might be used for supervisors and leads from all functions. Increasingly, organizations are seeking job-specific assessments, for example, an assessment designed specifically for a Chemist I in a particular company. Often competency assessments are completed by an employee (a self-rating) and by supervisors, and sometimes they are also completed by peers, direct reports, customers, and others, in which case they are called a *multirater* or a *360-degree review*.

In Figure 3-2, raters are presented with a competency description as well as four to ten related behaviors. They are asked to give an appropriate rating for the individual for the competency, using a rating scale. In this example, we see a five-point rating scale ranging from "little or no knowledge" to "expert." Raters also are encouraged to provide written comments to elaborate on the rationale behind their rating and/or make suggestions for further development of the person rated. Another variant (not shown) is to ask raters to give a separate rating for four to six behavioral descriptors for each competency, which are then compiled into an overall competency rating. Some competency rating instruments offer the option of evaluating more than one individual at a time, which saves time and tends to provide a wider distribution of ratings than if individuals are rated one at a time.

A simple competency rating assessment has many advantages. Foremost, it is far easier to use and much less expensive than a variety of other means of assessing competence, such as certifications, on-the-job observa-

Figure 3-2: Example of a Competency Assessment

STRATEGIC PLANNING AND FOCUS

STRATEGIC PLANNING AND FOCUS:
Demonstrate the ability to understand, create, communicate and implement sound business strategy. Make tactical and strategic adjustments where necessary.

Behavior

All Levels

- Analyze opportunities, threats, advantages and weaknesses based on current and future business trends
- Apply an understanding of "big picture" for the business in order to develop effective strategies
- Encourage others to think strategically
- Balance long-term strategic goals with short-term priorities
- Align projects and programs with the company's customer strategies and financial goals
- Effectively communicate and implement the strategic plans of the business

Competency 1 of 68: Go To

Assessee	DPL	Rating	Not Able to Rate	Comments	Rating Scale
					0 Little or no knowledge
Supervisor, Sam C.	3	4	☐	Edit	1 Novice
					2 Skilled
Bettis, Bert	2	3	☐	Edit	3 Advanced
					4 Expert

Rate the person(s) above on the competency described above.
If you haven't observed their behavior on this competency, check the *Not Able to Rate* column.

Scale Details

tions of workers, simulations, role plays, behavioral interviews, assessment centers, content or clinical testing, personal journals, and review boards. Simple competency assessments may require more administrative effort than performance reviews, especially when multiple raters are used for each individual, but multirater assessment software tools are readily available to assist with the process. With these tools, completing one or several job-specific competency assessments per year for every employee (maybe one related to current assignments, and a second related to career development) is not terribly daunting. Simple rating assessments are likely to be a big part of the strategy for most organizations today that wish to evaluate the competence of their talent pool. As with performance reviews, it is not our intent here to cover everything needed to know about simple competency ratings, but we do offer these recommendations:

■ As possible, employ job-specific competency models (which include technical competencies), not generic competency assessments, because job-specific assessments are more useful for making job assignments and also because the additional feedback they produce is more helpful to workers. Job-specific assessments typically include technical competencies that cannot be included in generic assessments, as well as core and cross-functional competencies.

■ Use an appropriate rating scale for competencies. Rating scales that look at whether an individual meets or exceeds expectations are appropriate for performance reviews, but not competency ratings. Most often, *level* of knowledge or skill scales (for example, "beginner," "novice," "competent," "advanced," "expert") are appropriate for cross-functional and technical competencies, and frequency-type scales (for example, "rarely," "sometimes," "usually," "almost always," and "always") are appropriate for values and traits or behaviors dependent more on motivation or commitment than on skill level (for example, accountability).

■ Competency ratings should be criterion-based, not normative-based, which simply means that people are compared to a standard, not to each other, and forced distributions are not used.

Certify Worker Competence

Organizations cannot always have high confidence in the accuracy of results obtained from simple competency ratings, in large part because they are subject to prevalent rater errors such as halo, leniency, first impression, and recency, which have been described extensively elsewhere. Therefore, it is worthwhile to consider more robust alternatives such as certifications, on-the-job observations, simulations, behavioral interviews, assessment centers, and knowledge or skill testing.

Certifications are increasingly being used by a wide variety of organizations and industries seeking a higher degree of confidence in the competence of their workforce. Our experience is that sometimes terms other than "certified" are preferred, such as verified, endorsed, tested, quality-assured, or accredited, but the intent is the same. Traditionally, certifications have been limited to industry-based tests, such as certified public accountant (CPA) or Microsoft Certified Systems Engineer. But that is changing. Organizations are increasingly developing their own internal certifications. This is an important development because industry-wide certifications are not available for many jobs and purposes. Certifications can provide highly valid and reliable results that give greater confidence to employers and customers alike than simple competency rating assessments. In turn, certified workers gain confidence, valuable skills, greater opportunity, potentially higher compensation, and pride in their accomplishments. *Accredited* certifications meet the high standards of outside bodies that are expert in structuring certifications.

At a minimum, certification programs must have these three elements:[1]

1. *Program Standards*: What knowledge or skill the program is certifying, coming from job analyses and stakeholder needs. For example, how to take a blood sample.

2. *Certification Requirements*: What people must do to become certified. For example, pass written and clinical tests, and be recertified every three years.

3. *Program Tests*: The assessment tools used to determine if candidates have met program standards, including valid, reliable ways of determining who has passed and who has not.

More mature certification programs also have the following:

1. *Preparation and Remediation Options:* Training for those who are preparing and support to help individuals succeed who did not initially pass the certification.

2. *Governance and Governance Bod6y:* Policies that result in a consistently high-quality program, and individuals to administer the policies.

3. *Administrative Practices:* Efficient implementation and record-keeping practices.

4. *Communications/Public Relations:* Information about the program required by all participants as well as positive press to encourage participation.

Clearly, certifications set the bar much higher than simple competency ratings. Here are a few examples of certifications:

■ A large supplier of industrial goods wishes to thrive in a market where there are many competitors, including some with lower prices, and many competitors that can offer the same brands and products. To differentiate itself and create a competitive advantage, the supplier has developed a number of proprietary tools that enable its sales force to calculate and communicate the cost savings clients will gain through buying through the supplier due to the breadth of its catalog and a number of special services. The required selling process is complex. In response, the supplier has developed a three-tier certification. The first tier is called *Foundational Knowledge*; salespersons take multiple-choice tests to confirm their knowledge retention from seven classes. The second tier is called *Performance*; salespersons are assessed on work samples they prepared for current prospects as well as role plays of typical situations (onsite observation of salespeople with clients was not a viable option). The third and final tier is called *Business Results*; salespersons are assessed on sales, documented cost savings, and required experience. Salespersons who pass the certification are rewarded with compensation, recognition, and special privileges. This certification is quite involved, but it does provide highly valid and comprehensive information on salesperson competence.

■ A pharmaceutical company wishes to control risks associated with manufacturing of drugs and diagnostic equipment. Therefore, it has developed work-specific certifications. The process is as follows:

Step 1: Learners are provided with access to detailed process documentation and various learning options.

Step 2: The learner decides (when he or she feels ready) to proceed with certification on a particular process or learning outcome.

Step 3: The certifier (either the supervisor or someone else who has been certified with the process) reviews for the learner what is required for the certification.

Step 4: The certifier uses a predeveloped assessment script to walk the learner through the learning demonstration process. The learner is asked to explain certain concepts and to demonstrate certain processes. Some of these are identified as *critical* (meaning the learner must do these) and some are *optional*. Choice of appropriate optional items serves to ensure that the certification is appropriate for the individual and means that the learner prepares for a wide possibility of questions or demos.

Step 5: The certifier provides reinforcing and corrective feedback as appropriate. If the learner passes, the certification is signed and dated. But if not, the learner undergoes further preparation before being assessed again.

■ A senior citizen care provider places great emphasis on its mission and values and has identified twenty related competencies, for example, alignment with values, change management, and tenacity. The company uses multirater assessments, but because of the importance of these particular competencies to the organization, it has gone an extra step and developed competency verifications. The company is an adherent to the philosophy that learning should be 70 percent on the job, 20 percent collaborative, and 10 percent formal learning, which is reflected in its verifications. Each verification describes (1) why the competency is important for the organization, (2) learning objectives divided into do/show and know/explain, (3) five to fifteen on-the-job-based activities where the competency can be learned, (4) available resources including subject matter experts and documentation, and (5) approaches to verify that the competency has been achieved. Although the approach sounds involved, the company has developed a process where each verification can be developed by using about two hours of SME time and three to four hours of the verification developer's time. Although a variety of alternatives for verification are offered (observation/demonstration, role plays, behavioral questions, multirater feedback, factual questions, journals, etc.), observation of one or more of the learning activities by one's supervisor is most often used. The supervisor looks for the individual's demonstration of four to eight predefined behaviors to determine whether the competency has been mastered.

Education: The Third Indicator of Talent

By education, we mean (1) compulsory and optional training provided by public and private schools and universities, as well as trade schools and executive education programs, some providing degrees and some providing certificates or licenses; and (2) corporate training programs delivered in a variety of manners such as in classrooms or through e-learning, books, workshops, collaboration, coaching, or on the job. Education is used as an indicator of competence, most often of broad competence on numerous foundational competencies. For example, it might be assumed that someone who has successfully completed a university degree program has developed reading skills sufficient for most assignments and at least basic competence in following directions, writing, analyzing, and solving problems. As successively advanced levels of education are completed, confidence in the *learning agility* (ability to understand and retain new information) of an individual increases. Education obtained from more prestigious learning institutions may be instructive because of higher entrance standards and more rigorous examinations.

Of course, it is widely understood that education is far from a perfect measure of competence. Two graduates from the same university with the same degree and a similar grade-point average may vary widely in their work performance. Formal education may not teach all the skills needed for work, such as interpersonal skills, or values such as accountability and integrity. Retention of important knowledge may vary widely, as well as the ability to apply the knowledge that has been learned in work settings. Given its faults, why not use other measures of competence instead? Education as a measure of competence does have these benefits:

- It may be the only measure of competence of a new, inexperienced worker where no track record of work performance is available.

- Education is a cost-effective measure of competence. Compared to other measures, it is relatively easy to measure and verify and can be used as a proxy measure for a potentially wide range of basic competencies important at work.

- Customers often have more confidence in individuals with higher levels of education. Certain levels of education are required for many professions such as medicine, education, and management.

The validity of education as a predictor of competence can be improved when the education received is similar to the work to be performed. It is advisable for an organization to track over time the success experienced with graduates of specific institutions or programs. Legal restrictions may apply to the use of education as a determinant of who is hired (for example, in *Griggs v. Duke Power Company*); it should not be used unless the education requirement is clearly job-related, both to stay clear of potential legal liability and because it will not help optimize the talent pool or workforce.

In addition to formal education, it is also useful to track professional training that individuals have received. You or other employers may have provided significant training to talent pool members, delivered internally or by external providers. Some individuals may have participated in much training over the years, so it may be necessary to focus on just a subset. Training received more recently may be most relevant. Also, individuals can be asked to list the most significant training they have received.

An online resume, curriculum vitae, or individual profile can be useful in maintaining information on the education, training, and experience of talent pool members (see Figure 3-3). Clearly you will want to encourage talent pool members to update this information regularly.

Figure 3-3: Education and Training Captured in an Online Employee Resume

Education ⊕ Add

College/University: Northwestern University
Degree: Masters - Business Administration
Date: May, 1995
✎ Edit Education   🗑 Delete Education

College/University: Loyola University
Degree: Bachelors of Arts, Sociology Major
Date: May, 1993
✎ Edit Education   🗑 Delete Education

Training ⊕ Add

Name: Work in staffing department for 90 days
Date: Sep, 2010
Note: This training was pulled automatically from your development plan.

Name: Strategies for Finding High Performers
Date: May, 2010
Note: This training was pulled automatically from your development plan.

Name: Hire With Your Head
Date: Apr, 2010
Note: This training was pulled automatically from your development plan.

Experience: The Fourth Indicator of Talent

By *experience*, we mean previous work done by individuals that is related to work you ask them to do for you. Information on work experience will generally be most useful in these circumstances:

- *It pertains to work done in the recent past.* Work done within the past one to two years is most instructive. Work done in the distant past, say twenty years earlier, may not be very helpful.

- *Internal work experience (work done for your organization) may be more useful than work performed externally for other organizations.* It is often easier to determine the relevance of internal work experience, and there is likely to be additional information available beyond just a description of the work.

- *Multiple, similar work experiences increase the confidence in an individual's competence more than a single work experience.* Similarly, five years of experience may be more instructive than one year.

- *In addition to knowing what a person did, you want to know the results.* Work experience with a performance review or another assessment is desirable.

- *Frank, credible references can be very useful in evaluating work experience, so it is helpful to request work references as well as permission to speak with the references.* Speaking with the ex-supervisor or sponsor of work previously done can provide much more detail than appears on a resume. Of course, two references are preferable to one. Even if you are unable to contact the references, having them may influence work candidates to be a little more accurate in describing their experience.

In addition to just collecting information that talent pool members provide you, it is advisable to ask them also about specific types of experience that are frequently needed by the organization. We refer to these as *critical qualifications* (see Figure 3-4). For example, it may be critical to the organization to have people with experience in international business, or opening new locations, or managing an acute care facility, or conducting an IT security audit. Identify the critical qualifications for the organization, and then ask talent pool members to identify which experiences they have, when and where they had them, and some details on what they did as well as what the results were.

Like education, experience is an indicator of competence. Therefore, it

Figure 3-4: Collection of Critical Qualification Experience

Edit Critical Qualifications

From the list of critical qualifications listed below, select critical qualifications that you possess. You can

✓	Critical Qualification	
☑	🔍1. Depth of Global Experience	✏I worked Tripoli ….
☑	🔍2. Cross cultural sensitivity	✏Experience in Lebanon with multipl
☑	🔍Acquisitions	✏I …
☐	🔍Completed Branch Mgr. Development Program	✏*No notes have been specified.*
☐	🔍Completion of Leadership Development Program	✏*No notes have been specified.*

is sometimes appropriate to use it in lieu of education, as is commonly done. Like education, experience can be an imperfect indicator of competence, but it is often a better indicator than education because it is usually more relevant to work, more recent, and more extensive than information on education. Recall that our purpose is to identify persons who consistently achieve desired results. Experience is a very important part of the data we need to create mature talent pools.

Personal Preferences: The Fifth Indicator of Talent

Personal preferences include the type of work a person likes to do, functional areas of interest, preferred amount of interaction with others, decision making, working conditions, geographic locations, preferred hours, and more. Clearly, we are more likely to attract and retain people if we can more closely match job assignments with their preferences. People tend to like what they do well (for example, interaction with others) or conditions that play to their strengths (for example, low or high job structure), so matching personal preferences and job characteristics may also result in better qualified workers.

You can begin by asking individuals about their specific job or assignment preferences. Let them select all that interests them, possibly ranked in order of preference. It is also useful to inquire about their interests based on the demographics of the organization. If you have offices in New York, London, Sydney, and Munich, which of these locations interests them? Would they be interested in work done by IT, administration, accounting, HR, or other functions? This information will help you narrow the search when assignments become available.

Job characteristics describe a potentially wide variety of job design elements that typically by themselves are neither inherently good nor inherently bad, but that affect people differently (see Figure 3-5). For example, some people like the opportunity to make decisions, while others do not want the responsibility that goes along with it. Some are amenable and even want to travel, while others do not. Other common types of job characteristics that can be used to match workers and assignments include amount of interaction with others, amount of job structure (specified ways the job must be done versus deciding oneself how to do the work), frequency of performance feedback (from every few hours to every few months), stability of job priorities (from stable to changing priorities every day), job pace (from relaxed to rushed), physical requirements (from none to strenuous), and amount of interaction with senior leaders. Job characteristics can be selected from any reputable career or vocational selection instrument. We have found the work descriptors of John Holland to be quite useful.

In addition to using an instrument to match individual preferences and job characteristics, one of the tried-and-true methods for identifying worker fit problems is to let potential assignees react to a *realistic job preview*. This can begin with a good job or assignment description. If you wish, there are additional steps that can provide individuals with a clear view of what life will be like if they take a given assignment, such as meeting their potential supervisor and team members, talking to former or current job incumbents, or observing or even taking on the assignment on a trial basis. When problems are identified during the realistic job preview process, it may be possible to deal with them up front, or the assignees may be willing to cope with the issues when they know in advance they are part of the assignment.[2]

Figure 3-5: Example of Personal Preferences for Job Characteristics

Job Characteristics Interested In   ✎ Edit

Administrative Burden:	5 - Highly Administrative
Analysis:	3 - Mixed Analysis & Action
Concreteness:	2 - Primarily Abstract
Frequency of Reviews:	1 - Very Infrequent Review
Independence:	1 - Very Little Independence
Influence on Others:	3 - Moderate Influence
Interaction:	5 - High Interaction
Interaction with Sr. Mgmt.:	4 - Frequent Interaction with Sr. Mgmt.
Multi-Tasking:	1 - Little or No Multi-Tasking
Pace:	3 - Fast-Paced
Physical Requirements:	1 - Little or No Physical Requirements
Stability of Priorities:	4 - Stable Priorities
Structure:	4 - Primarily Structured
Teamwork:	5 - Very Significant Teamwork Required
Time Spent on Computer:	4 - Between 2–4 hours per day
Travel:	1 - Seldom or Never Travel
Variety of Tasks:	3 - Moderate Job Variety

Other Indicators of Talent and Worker Fit

Although past performance may be the single best predictor we have of an individual's future performance, it is far from perfect, particularly for new assignments that differ markedly from previous assignments. That is why we recommend also collecting information on competence, education, experience, and personal preferences. And yet even with all this information, it is quite possible that a stellar performer in one role in 2011 could turn out to be a miserable failure in a different role in 2012, even if all our information has led us to believe that the individual was perfect for the assignment. What happened? There are numerous possibilities. Perhaps:

- The worker has reacted badly to changes in the compensation or benefits package and has therefore adjusted his or her output downward according to what he or she feels is equitable.

- The management style of the new supervisor just does not mesh well with the style under which the worker flourishes.

- The worker is familiar with older technologies, but those are changing rapidly and he or she is not motivated to put in the effort to learn the required new technology.

- The worker's income needs have increased dramatically and he or she has taken on too many other assignments to meet financial obligations. Now the worker simply lacks sufficient energy to sustain work throughout a normal workday.

Changes in supervision, rewards and compensation, and personal circumstances are just a few of the frequently changing situational factors that could affect future performance. Job characteristic preferences touch on a few of these situational factors, but there are dozens of others. So what is the ROI in expanding data collection beyond the five indicators of talent? When do we reach the point of diminishing returns where further data-collection effort isn't justified?

We believe that the most practical approach is to concentrate on conscientiously and accurately assessing the five indicators of talent that we have discussed. Most importantly, they should provide enough information about workers to make reasonably accurate predictions about whether they can complete an assignment well. Second, they are relatively stable compared to situational factors that can and do change frequently. Finally, these indicators, particularly performance history, do give us some insight into whether situational factors are likely to derail an individual.

Performance history becomes increasingly valuable when we have a history of performance over a period of years and many assignments because in most cases, workers are exposed over time to myriad conditions, such as different supervisors, changes in technology, different customers, changes in work design, and changes in personal circumstances. Despite these inevitable changes, some workers perpetually make the needed adjustments, overcome challenges, and consistently perform effectively. What they bring to work that makes them successful may sometimes be a "black box" of talent and experience that is not well-understood but nevertheless suggests that they can be counted on to make valuable contributions despite the circumstances.

We are not advocating that obvious situational "red flags" be ignored. It is best to address these issues (for example, a weak supervisor or negative culture) directly, rather than try to find a worker that can still be effective despite the challenges. Still, a consistently strong performance history is an important indicator of future success when situational issues can't be addressed.

The Limitations of Measuring Workers by "Potential"

Although most organizations have not yet developed mature talent pools, many do have succession pools, and performance and *potential* (not competence) are the metrics they most commonly use to review their talent using the familiar 9-Box[3] (see Figure 3-6). Talent pools and succession pools share many similarities. Both provide a roster of individuals who have

Figure 3-6: Traditional Succession-Planning 9-Box

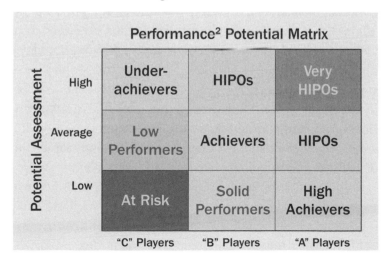

been prequalified for assignments and both are essentially insurance plans for the future. In each case, pool members may or may not receive the assignments for which they have been qualified. Granted, with a talent pool, it may be more likely that members already have experience in the assignments for which they are backups (for example, few succession chart members slotted as backups for the CEO are likely to have previous CEO experience). But even with a talent pool, individuals are asked to perform assignments that are new and unique.

We prefer to use the five talent indicators we have described, not potential, to populate talent and succession pools. We recommend using performance and competence as the two dimensions for a 9-Box. We believe these measures are superior for predicting future performance, and they don't carry the possible liabilities associated with measures of potential.

Arguments can certainly be made for using potential. First, it is already in widespread use. Second, advocates of potential point out that organizations are strewn with failures due to the "Peter Principle"; that is, organizations tend to regularly promote successful workers until they finally reach a level where they are no longer competent. There are plenty of examples of strong individual contributors who have been promoted to supervisory positions and simply lacked the competencies to be successful in that new role. The impact of the Peter Principle is magnified because besides selecting someone who is ineffective for an important position, a strong performer has been removed from another important role. Also, organizations with a limited talent pool (essentially just their current workforce) do not have prepared backups to backfill all their roles. Without strong backups and typically without the data needed to accurately predict other assignments an individual can perform successfully, an estimate of potential may be considered better than nothing.

From a historical perspective, Peter Cappelli[4] helps us understand in part how and why *potential* came into use as a predictor of performance. Cappelli notes that high-potential programs were created after World War II because there was an insufficient supply of corporate leadership talent to meet the needs of fast-growing economies. Hiring leadership talent away from competitors was not a viable option, so organizations had little choice in the short term except to develop the talent they needed themselves. Leadership development programs were rigorous, comprehensive, multiyear commitments. High-profile speakers, retreats, and executive development programs at prestigious locales were costly. Naturally it was advantageous to select program participants who had high potential to negotiate the program successfully, advance to leadership positions, and then provide a good ROI.

Various measures of leadership potential were developed, but they were almost never validated in companies. After all, only candidates who scored high on potential were selected for high-potential programs, and test validation would have required that candidates from varying levels of test performance be accepted. Then it would have been necessary to track the careers of each individual (keeping those who were not initially performing well in the program to complete the research) and correlate low- and high-potential candidates with one or several measures of actual performance. It is understandable that few if any organizations would be willing to do that, even though it would have provided greater confidence that the right candidates were being selected and enhanced legal defensibility of their leadership candidate selections.

Some tests of potential probably did help predict successful completion of the leadership training. It was common to include a measure of intelligence as part of a battery of tests, and years of using such tests in university admissions have proven that intelligence is one of the best predictors of academic performance (that is, successful completion of training). Unfortunately, intelligence is not nearly as good a predictor of success after training.

Besides the lack of validation, we see numerous difficulties with measuring potential to populate talent or succession pools, to determine future job assignments, and even to determine which workers will receive scarce investments in further development. Here are some of the problems:

■ There is no agreed-on set of traits (called potential) that produces valid, reliable predictions of future performance across a wide variety of conditions. Some qualities may be necessary but are not sufficient as predictors. The problem is the same as that of defining the critical elements of leadership. Despite decades of research on leaders, dozens of leadership models still abound, and the right leadership model appears to depend on a unique interaction of the challenges being faced and the complete package of competencies brought by a leader. For example, a leader with a dominating style may be successful if that is combined with a crisis and a high level of personal credibility, but that does not mean that being high on dominance will be successful for a different leader facing different circumstances.

■ In practice today, many of the measures used to assess potential are very weak. Often they are little more than the impressions of others, with each evaluator using different criteria. For example the height of a male has been used either explicitly or as an unspoken qualification, with taller males given credit because it is believed that they create greater presence.

■ Typically, a *single rating* of potential is determined. Someone with considerable potential for one job, however, may have little or no potential for another. Some have great potential to be good engineers, and others have potential to be professional athletes, but it does not necessarily follow that someone who has high potential for one assignment will also have potential for another.

■ There are plenty of persons who have been motivated to overcome deficits that might have appeared to limit their potential. Drive, hard work, and goal orientation can make up for deficits in other areas.

■ Telling people they do not have high potential (even if they are assured that they are "valued performers") is divisive and discouraging and can result in lowered commitment or even undesired turnover.

■ A high percentage (about half) of organizations that give potential ratings keep them secret, often for very solid reasons, but this creates other difficulties. Secret ratings make it much more difficult to engage high potentials in their own continued development. Secrecy leads to worker uncertainty about their perceived value and future in the organization, and it prevents an opportunity to clear up any misunderstandings about one's capabilities.

In real-life settings, there are too many factors and too much complexity to consistently and accurately predict potential. We might consider five to ten factors, but dozens could be important. Intelligence and learning agility might be valuable and statistically correlated to high performance in leadership jobs. However, deficits in various areas of "emotional" intelligence can easily derail intelligent, learning-agile individuals from leadership success. Further, as we noted earlier, seemingly positive or negative competencies can interact with each other in unique ways that are hard to predict. Some proponents of potential may argue that even a weak measure of potential is better than none, but our point of view is that the five talent indicators we have described are as good or better predictors of performance and they do not carry the liabilities of potential.

Availability of Workers

We have described the data that need to be collected to predict future performance. Worker *availability* is another important variable to track. If we do not track the availability of talent pool members, we of course risk the liabilities and expenses that come with going outside our talent pool for needed workers. On the other hand, it is worse to be overstaffed. A mature talent pool enables you to have sufficient talent available to meet a variety of circumstances, *but not pay for workers when you do not need them.*

For example, a large international consulting company responds to many requests for proposals (RFPs) for potential client engagements. The company does not know which of these opportunities will eventually turn into work and is not willing to bear the costs of hiring the talent to staff the work ahead of time and have that talent "sit on the bench" waiting for the engagement, particularly when it may never occur. Instead, at the time the RFP response is prepared, the company contacts qualified individuals from its talent pool who are not full-time staff members and asks them if they would be interested in working on the project if the contract is secured. Those who are interested sign a contract that states that if they are called by the company, they agree to be available for work within twenty-four hours. No excuses.

Binding contracts can ensure that talent pool members will be available, but in general talent pools are very fluid. At any moment, members of the meticulously constructed, mature talent pool may sign a binding contract with another organization. Or accept a full-time job with someone else. Or take off five years to raise a family. Or retire. Or move to Alberta, Canada, where bodies are needed and salaries are high to mine tar sands. Availability is important beyond scenarios involving contingent workers. Even full-time employees have limits as to how many assignments they can assume at one time. Many organizations have found themselves in trouble with their replacement planning when they have slotted the same talented individual as the number one backup for too many assignments. A talent pool might appear to be more than sufficient to handle work needs, but in reality, due to the unavailability of workers, you may have a shortage of available talent.

Constant communication is critical to confirm and reconfirm worker availability and *interests.* But communication is not nearly enough. *Strong relationships* are also required. Social media can be effectively employed. Increasingly, organizations are developing active "alumni" networks. For example, McKinsey & Company[5] report having an alumni network of nearly 23,000 individuals. Although the alumni organization serves those who have left McKinsey, this network is also meant to serve current firm members; it builds lasting relationships between alumni and the firm and colleagues currently working at the firm. The company states:

> People who join McKinsey find themselves part of a unique culture, shaped by shared values and a desire to help clients make substantial improvements in their performance. When consultants leave, *their connection to our firm and their former colleagues remains strong.*

How can a company estimate how much available talent is needed? For a given job, role, or assignment companies can measure average turnover, historical fill times, and the likelihood of turnover of current incumbents (that is, retention risk). *Role criticality* is another consideration—that is, how many days it could remain open before the organization would face unacceptable costs or consequences. Based on these and other related data, the organization can determine the number of currently available backups required for each role or position.

Build a Cost-Effective Workforce

Few if any will argue against the benefits of keeping labor costs under careful control and reducing them where it can be done reasonably without jeopardizing results. Providing cost-effective workers is one of the keys to optimizing talent pools and achieving an optimal work-worker match. This process involves estimating labor costs associated with using different resources within the talent pool, estimating benefits, calculating ROI, comparing the alternatives, and then making the best choice.

It is not difficult to roughly estimate the cost of a given full-time employee. We might base the estimate on salary, benefits, and overhead. We might start with salary, then add actual costs of benefits or a multiplier (for example, benefits might add 35 percent additional costs over and above salary), and then add a multiplier or share per employee of company overhead. The precision of the calculation can be enhanced, if desired. Calculating the cost of a contingent worker is similar but often easier because of fewer benefits and less overhead.

The process becomes a bit more difficult from that point. Determining which workers are truly most "cost-effective" looks to be relatively simple, but in some circumstances it is not straightforward. For example, imagine ABC Software Company located in a country such as the United States with relatively high salaries. ABC may follow the path of many other software companies and outsource some or even all of its software development to companies in other countries. Whereas the cost of hiring a competent software development consultant (a nonemployee) in the United States might range roughly from $60 to $200 per hour, the cost to hire a software developer in India might range from $10 to $35 per hour, roughly one-third to a quarter of the cost in the United States. Surely there are large savings to be gained by ABC from outsourcing the job to India, right? It is not easy to be certain, however, as there are a number of other variables to consider.

The hourly wage of the offshore developer is not the only associated cost; there is hidden overhead. To outsource work, it is often necessary to spend significantly more time having local staff carefully specify the work requirements before the offshore developer begins. Additionally, it may be necessary for ABC to do extensive project management. Further, one local developer will likely need to participate in frequent meetings with the outsourced developers, telling them how to reproduce defects and where to find particular tables. Time differences can also be a problem. When workdays do not overlap much or at all, there is limited time to discuss issues, and an overseas developer may wait twenty-four hours to get an answer to a critical question versus five minutes if the person with the answer were at the workplace. Even different languages or different accents can slow communication, and cultural differences can cause misunderstandings. In sum, the true cost of using the overseas developer may be far more than the $10 to $35 advertised rate.

Besides cost, there is the issue of output (benefit), which together with cost is used to calculate the ROI of the developer. In virtually every job, some workers excel and far outperform other workers. For years, industrial-organizational psychologists have used a rough rule of thumb that, on average for most jobs, someone performing at the 80th percentile for his group will produce approximately twice as much as someone performing at the 20th percentile. For some jobs, such as software developers, research shows that the difference in output between more effective and less effective performers can be much greater than double the productivity; strong software developers appear to produce ten times as much as programmers at the other end of the spectrum, even when experience is controlled for in the research.

Although there are plenty of challenges in calculating the costs, the benefits, and ultimately the ROI of different workforce alternatives, rough estimates are better than none. In general, the five talent indicators along with wages, benefits, and overhead will be helpful in selecting which resources, internal or external, domestic or international, can best meet work needs. We anticipate that soon tools to make these estimates easily and frequently, in fact before each assignment, will be readily available.

Be Strategic in How and When You Verify the Talent Pool

Talent pool optimization is a process for qualifying talent you expect to need instead of waiting and being left with inferior choices, which is a bit like qualifying a sales lead first so that effort is not wasted later. Ideally, if we had unlimited time and resources, we could identify talent for every likely future need. That is, we would know in advance exactly where to find the talent we need and that the talent was qualified, available, and cost-effective. However, having identified talent is more critical in some circumstances than in others. For example, *when* the proverbial pipe bursts (and eventually it will), we may pay a large price (maybe the loss of a major customer) if we have to spend time looking for a qualified, available plumber. There are other assignments that are less urgent or where the effort involved with identifying replacements or resources just is not worth the effort. Further, unknown backups may be acceptable in cases where we know the supply is plentiful.

For most organizations, there will never be enough resources to implement talent pool optimization for all jobs. Although we have spent the majority of this chapter discussing best practices for optimizing the talent pool, for many organizations the process will begin (and may end) with small steps in the right direction. Some movement in the right direction is better than none. Further, it will take some time to optimize the talent pool, and it makes sense to begin with the most critical jobs, and successively work through the remainder as resources allow.

Talent can be qualified in various ways with differing degrees of rigor depending on the nature of the work. It is helpful to consider the proper level of talent qualification for different talent pool members, choosing from the following three levels: *verified, identified,* or *assumed.* For example, suppose we decide we need five software developers with a specific skill set. *Verification* is the highest level of qualification. To verify that the candidates are well-qualified, we can use the five talent indicators discussed earlier, that is, performance history, competence, education, experience, and personal preferences, or a subset of these five. Alternatively, we might be satisfied with doing a little bit of research and *identifying* sufficient numbers of people in our talent pool with some form of the job title "software developer" and confirming that we will have access to them. Even labor statistics might be used to identify software developer availability. Finally, a third alternative is to *assume* that the needed talent supply will be available when needed. That is, we may have little or no advance information on qualified, available, affordable software developers, but we might be satisfied with beginning our search for the needed talent at the time the need arises. The third approach may appear reckless, but it is clearly the most widely used approach today, and it may be a reasonable choice when talent is plentiful, internal staffing resources are scarce and/or assignments are pedestrian. This third alternative is the only one available for any talent needs we do not anticipate in advance.

Within one organization, it is common to find instances of verified, identified, or assumed talent supply. Many organizations have planned replacements for their senior leadership positions. Increasingly organizations are identifying other jobs that are not part of senior leadership but are critical and deserve in-depth, advanced attention because vacancies or unqualified talent are too costly. For example, a healthcare organization may decide to verify nurses and radiologists, identify IT staff, but do nothing in advance until a need arises for additional in-house patient transport.

Sourcing Talent for the Talent Pool

Organizations (and their talent pools) in the twentieth century were built on the familiar and pervasive model of full-time employee workforces, sometimes with augmentation by a small group of outside consultants and specialists. The full-time employee model has many advantages. Workers gain a steady, reliable income that matches well with ongoing personal or family financial obligations. The employing organization "owns" a worker's time during the workweek. Long-term workers often have invaluable knowledge and experience, and many who have struggled with the use of alternative workers believe that full-time workers are inherently more motivated and engaged than part-timers or contractors (we will explore the relative benefits of full-time versus contract workers in detail in chapter 6, as well as other implications for workers as the use of the full-time employee model decreases).

Granted, there have long been some organizations that rely on nontraditional workforces so that they can be rapidly ramped up or down in size. Key among these are industries or occupations whose workload varies predictably. These include migrant farm workers who help harvest crops, amusement parks or camps that staff up during the summer, accounting firms that are busier during tax season, and retailers who are busier during holiday seasons. Other organizations, such as healthcare organizations, commonly have ebbs and flows of work even if the timing cannot be easily predicted.

Today, many more organizations are straying from the traditional full-time, local workforce model and are using a variety of alternative workers, ranging from a retiree who has returned to work part-time to a worker located on the other side of the globe. For example, telephone centers that support sales or provide helpdesk support are increasingly outsourced to take advantage of lower-cost but highly educated workers in other countries. Many alternative workers are *contingent* workers. By *contingent*, we mean those who work when there is a clear need for them. In other words, they are just-in-time, just-when-needed workers, whether that means helping out during periods of particularly heavy workloads, such as extra accountants during tax season, or bringing in a specialist such as an intellectual property attorney.

In many economies, work has morphed from being primarily agricultural and/or manufacturing to white-collar and computer-based. Meanwhile, e-mail, instant messaging, low-cost telephone, web-meeting software, and work group collaboration tools like SharePoint make it easy for workers from around the globe to collaborate. Further, online outsourcing portals such as Elance make it quick, easy, and cost-effective to find temporary, qualified outside assistance. Temporary work agencies such as Manpower Inc. are flourishing, and many new temporary work agencies with a particular specialty, for example, human resources and accounting, are emerging. The bottom line is that organizations have many more options today to make effective use of contingent workers. Given the many new opportunities for building the talent pool as well as the fact that competitors are utilizing these new options, which in many cases cut costs and increase competitiveness, it is advisable for virtually all organizations to at least consider the question, *"What is the right mix of full-time employees and contingent workers for us?"* The following case study shows the innovative approaches used by accounting firm McGladrey[6] to handle a large increase of work during tax season.

McGLADREY (U.S. PROVIDERS OF ASSURANCE, TAX, AND CONSULTING SERVICES)

Many organizations have peaks and valleys in work demand. For accounting and tax firms, like McGladrey & Pullen, LLP, and RSM McGladrey, the peak is "busy season," which lasts from January through mid-April in the United States. Busy season has been compared by accountants to a marathon or 1,001-mile bicycle race.

During busy season, workload significantly increases. Thomas Green, partner with McGladrey and Pullen, LLP, estimates that during busy season the workload is approximately 30 to 50 percent more than during non–busy season (see Figure 3-7). Other than staffing up with a larger, full-time workforce that can meet busy season demand (and in the process being saddled with excessive labor costs, particularly when the workload normalizes at the end of the busy season), how does McGladrey get over the hump? It employs a number of effective strategies.

Figure 3-7: Seasonality of Accounting and Tax Industry

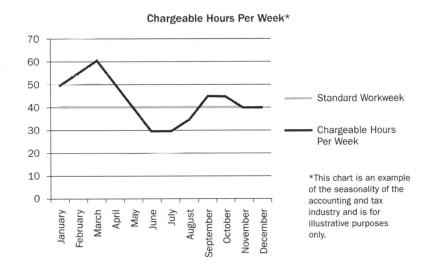

Chargeable Hours Per Week*

——— Standard Workweek

——— Chargeable Hours Per Week

*This chart is an example of the seasonality of the accounting and tax industry and is for illustrative purposes only.

■ *Seasonal Workers.* McGladrey uses well-known, proven performers in this role. These individuals are typically former full-time employees with a lot of experience, sometimes more than fifteen years. Some have left their full-time accounting careers so that they could devote more time to their families or other passions.

McGladrey knows that busy season lies ahead each year, and it does not leave the availability of desirable seasonal workers to chance nor does it wait to contact them until a few weeks before the need. There are informal touch points with these seasonal employees throughout the year, with more concentrated discussions regarding timing and scheduling starting each fall. Granted, after eight months away from work, skills can become a little rusty, so McGladrey in some instances provides seasonal staff with refresher training before busy season begins. This training also allows the workers to meet their continuing education requirement to maintain their CPA license, making them more valuable. Seasonal worker transition is also eased by carefully selecting work assignments that are aligned with the worker's former experience. Where possible, the seasonal worker is assigned the same clients from year to year. Also, since the same audit and tax software is used from year to year, working with it is akin to riding a bicycle—it comes back very quickly. Learning a few new features each year requires minimal effort.

McGladrey is considerate of the flexible needs of these workers. Although it is busy season, it doesn't mean that worker circumstances have changed since they stopped working full-time. For example, if they need to be home by a certain time, McGladrey is supportive of their need to be on the 4:40 train each day. McGladrey has found that seasonal workers with more limited work time often compensate with superior time-management skills, and productivity does not suffer.

■ *Extended Workweeks.* Accountants and tax professionals know that long workdays during busy season may be a requirement of the job. McGladrey generally expects employees to extend their work hours as needed to serve the needs of their clients during this time or any time throughout the year.

■ *Work/Life Balance.* McGladrey recognizes the sacrifices individuals make for the firm, and in turn it wants to help employees better integrate the demands of work and home. It supports flexible work arrangements that ultimately benefit clients, workers, and the firm. McGladrey offers a flexible work option (FWO), where work hours are "annualized" during the school year. For example, FWOs often reduce the workweek schedule of employees who choose to spend more time with their children during the summers, when they are out of school. In other cases, people work at home or at a local office that minimizes their commute.

■ *Interns.* Depending on their geographic location, different McGladrey offices and practices have identified certain key schools with strong accounting programs as places to regularly recruit talent. Many of the students want to complete a master's degree, and significant internship hours are required. McGladrey professionals meet the students early in their careers by sponsoring presentations at the selected universities or social events. Again, frequent touch points throughout the year help maintain relationships with these students.

Internships are offered to more advanced students with strong resumes who want to gain practical audit and tax experience. Once interns begin work, they are treated similarly, with the same high expectations, as entry-level hires during busy season. They work until late in the evening along with the rest of their engagement teams. The interns enjoy the camaraderie associated with being treated like any other valued team member and they are paid very well compared to other types of interns. Additionally, those who have performed effectively often secure full-time job offers to join McGladrey after graduation.

McGladrey has found (as many other firms have discovered) that utilizing interns is a low-risk way to find and validate talent. Working directly with the interns, McGladrey can determine which interns have a strong work ethic as well as those that can successfully deal with the challenges that young staff members face as they prove themselves serving clients.

■ *Secondees.* McGladrey brings accounting and tax professional secondees (*secondees* are persons who are temporarily transferred to other employment) over to the United States from countries such as South Africa, New Zealand, and Australia (their busy season is opposite that in North America). Generally these are senior staff level individuals with three to five years of experience who have an interest in living in another country for three to four months. Why bear the costs of bringing these individuals to the United States? The lost revenue associated with not being able to staff a project is far greater than the cost of bringing over qualified individuals. Unlike outsource workers, secondees interact directly and locally with the supervisor and can therefore be assigned to tasks that are not as cut-and-dried. Some secondees return three or four years in a row, which gives McGladrey a very good understanding of their strengths and what assignments are most appropriate. McGladrey also sends some professionals overseas to RSM International member firms after the busy season, thereby reducing staff at a time when the workload is less. These two-way exchanges increase mutual understanding of needs and increase the success of the talent exchange in future years.

Both interns and secondees are onboarded to the organization much like a full-time employee would be. The orientation includes an introduction to the firms and their history as well as an education of the systems and protocols required by McGladrey. For example, these include review of time and expense entry, online file tools, navigation of the firm's intranet, etc. In addition to the administrative orientation, each intern and secondee will also get line-of-business training and in most cases industry training by the industry team he or she is assigned to. At the end of the day the takeaways from training along with the camaraderie of the people who went through orientation together will remain for years to come.

■ *Risk Management.* Certainly McGladrey could attempt to absorb the extra work during busy season using only current staff. However, in recent years risk and exposure have increased for professional services firms. Firms have faced investor lawsuits and a loss of reputation, and have even been driven out of business when high-profile clients have unexpectedly failed. Further, government agencies have set standards that must be maintained. An audit firm cannot just throw anyone at a task. It pays to ensure that top-flight talent is assigned to each project.

■ *Process Documentation.* McGladrey maintains standard programs (an extensive database of policies, procedures, and templates of letters and communications). Extensive documentation of processes is key and ensures that work will be completed at a uniformly high level. It also is a great advantage to have this documentation when using nontraditional workers. Documentation allows such workers to get up to speed quickly with required approaches, and to complete work in an acceptable fashion that is consistent with the way a full-time employee would complete work or communicate with a client.

■ *Process Improvement.* McGladrey constantly reviews business processes and tries to determine if work can be done more effectively and efficiently. It also looks at impediments (what held McGladrey up last year) and considers whether it can further utilize technology to automate a process or get better information from a client.

In summary, due to busy season, McGladrey knows it will face uneven work demand each year. Rather than utilizing traditional staffing methods for the peak demand, McGladrey strategically sources alternative employee talent from a variety of carefully managed programs. In the process, it realizes other advantages such as identification of future full-time talent and cross-pollination of ideas from its talented colleagues all over the world.

We are *not* suggesting that the use of alternative workers is a panacea. For example, some outsourced functions fail to meet expectations and ultimately are brought back in-house. The use of alternative workers often requires arduous contract negotiations, detailed work specifications, and increased project management. However, lessons are being learned, and many organizations are developing greater facility with using alternative workers. We foresee a future where many organizations will have talent pools primarily made up of resources that are neither full-time nor employees.

Chapter Summary

In this chapter, we have discussed how to build a talent pool, that is, the ways of assessing, monitoring, and finding talent qualified, available, and cost-effective for our assignments. In chapter 4 we move to a discussion of places to source candidates for our talent pool. For more than half a century, the full-time employee workforce has been considered the first and sometimes the only choice for many assignments. Today there are many alternative sources of talent that can increase organizational agility, improve talent, and result in cost advantages. Chapter 4 explores alternative workers in detail.

OPTIMIZE THE WORKFORCE

SEVERAL QUESTIONS should be considered when the goal is to optimize the workforce. First, what are the most important *core competencies* (that is, greatest strategic strengths) of the organization? How can staffing enhance that strength to achieve work results that meet or exceed customer or stakeholder requirements? Those are *strategic questions* that will enhance the organization's effectiveness. Second, once the profile has been prepared of the ideal work product or service, how can an organization's leaders work backward to staff for specific positions required to do that work? Third, how can the staff skills or competencies required to achieve that ideal work product or service best be acquired on a timely basis? These questions are *tactical questions* that will enhance the organization's efficiency.

Strategic issues surge to the forefront as decision makers consider how to compete with other organizations for market share, economic results, customer satisfaction, or other measures of successful organizational performance. It is a long-term challenge to match up, through creative methods, the quantity (head count) and quality (talents/competencies) of the organization's collective human capital to achieve successful results.

The tactical issues grow most important when decision makers ponder what to do about filling one job vacancy resulting from organizational growth or worker departure. Many organizational leaders today assume that they may need an inner core of so-called permanent staff and an outer core of other people—such as vendors, consultants, contingent workers, or temps—on which to download some tasks that are more cost-effectively handled by others. This is called the "hole in the doughnut" approach to staffing (see Figure 4-1).

In reality, however, many organizations may not need a large permanent staff if the real goal is to get the work accomplished or achieve the work results desired by customers or other important stakeholders. It is, after all, costly to maintain a full-time permanent staff. Often these workers qualify for benefits as well as wages or salaries.

Having said that, it is worth noting that there can be occasions when a permanent staff is necessary. Consider:

- How much competitive advantage will be gained and sustained by having full-time workers devoted to meeting the special needs of customers, clients, or other stakeholders?

- How steep is the learning curve involved in learning how to moot the unique needs of customers, clients, or stakeholders?

Figure 4-1: The "Hole in the Doughnut" Approach to Staffing

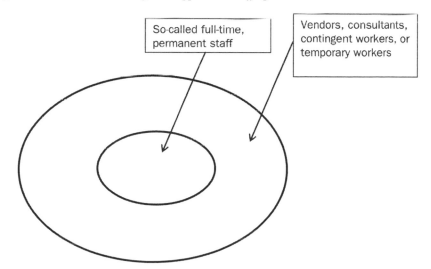

- How steep is the learning curve involved in learning how to deliver services or make products that meet or exceed unique customer, client, or stakeholder requirements?

- How steep is the learning curve to master the organization's corporate culture ("the way we do things here") or work processes ("the unique way we want to deliver our services or make our products to match customer needs")?

If the answers to these questions indicate that cost savings or customer satisfaction can result from maintaining a cadre of full-time staff, then that might be more appropriate than using other, more creative ways to get the work done. Still, it is to be questioned *how many or what percentage of workers* really need to be full-time to meet or exceed unique customer expectations or requirements in service delivery or in product manufacture.

This chapter introduces the notion of alternative staffing approaches. Many organizational leaders have experimented with such alternatives over the years with a view to dramatically cutting wage and benefit costs while maintaining (or even enhancing) service or product quality. But it is to be debated just how systematically they consider the options. What model may guide these choices systematically? What options exist to deliver services or make products? What are the relative advantages and disadvantages of each option? How can staffing gaps be closed? What staffing approaches can be selected to align talent to organizational objectives? And if these approaches are considered and lead to new ways of staffing for work, what frequently asked questions are likely to emerge by leaders and workers?

A Model to Guide Systematic Staffing Choices

Examine the model appearing in Figure 4-2. Then consider the description of the model appearing below.

Meet Customer or Stakeholder Requirements

The goal of this step is to agree to reach agreement on what outputs and outcomes are sought from the organization. The organization's leaders may assume they know what customers or stakeholders want. While leaders' viewpoints are important, assumptions are not as good as facts collected from the customers or other stakeholders themselves. Nothing is certain until some effort is made to systematically investigate those expectations.

Figure 4-2: A Model to Guide Systematic Staffing Choices

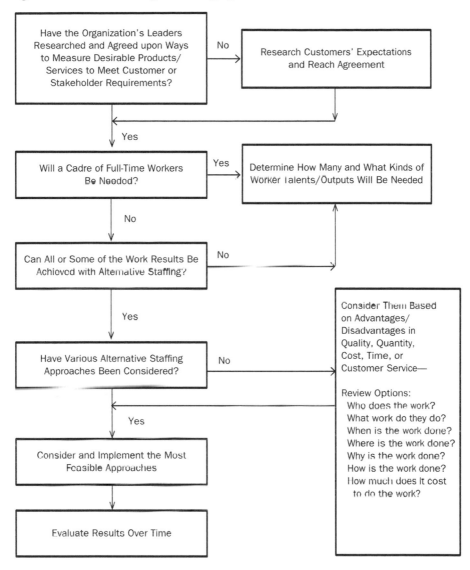

What do customers want most? How do they assess their own needs and wants? What do other stakeholders—such as suppliers, distributors, vendors, or others—need or want, and how do they clarify their expectations? How can their expectations be specifically measured for services and/or products according to time, cost, quality, quantity, or satisfaction?

The same issues should also be addressed for each part of the organization. What are the products and services offered by each functional part of the organization? What are the core competencies of each part? Who are the customers and stakeholders served by each component of the organization, and how can the expectations of its customers and/or stakeholders be specifically measured for services and/or products according to time, cost, quality, quantity, or satisfaction?

Research Customers' Expectations and Reach Agreement

Identify who are the customers and who are the key stakeholders of the organization. Go to them and find out what affects their level of satisfaction with the organization's products and/or services. What do they like most? What do they like least? Why do they like what they like? Why do they not like what they do not like? What do they believe distinguishes the organization and its products from the organization's competitors? Use the worksheet appearing in Figure 4-3 to organize the leaders' thinking about these issues. The same approach can also be used to explore similar questions for each part of the organization, as indicated in Figure 4-4.

Figure 4-3: A Worksheet to Research Customers' Expectations and Reach Agreement

Directions:	Use this worksheet to organize the thinking of customers and other stakeholders about the organization. Pose the questions below to customers and stakeholders. Then summarize their responses and feed them back to the organization's leaders. Add more paper if necessary.	
Questions		**Answers**
1	Who are the organization's customers? Describe them as specifically as possible.	
2	Who are the organization's stakeholders? Describe suppliers, distributors, and others as specifically as possible.	
3	How satisfied are customers with the organization? What do they like most about the organization? What do they like least? Why?	
4	How satisfied are stakeholders with the organization? What do they like most about the organization? What do they like least? Why?	
5	What do customers and stakeholders believe distinguishes the organization and its products from the organization's competitors?	

Figure 4-4: A Worksheet to Research Customers' Expectations and Reach Agreement in One Organizational Component

Directions:	Use this worksheet to organize the thinking of customers and other stakeholders about ONE part of the organization—such as one division, department, or work team. Pose the questions below to the external and internal customers and stakeholders of that organization's component. Then summarize their responses and feed them back to the organization's leaders. Add more paper if necessary.	
Questions		**Answers**
1	Who are the internal and external customers *of this part of the organization*? Describe the customers as specifically as possible and how each customer group is served.	
2	Who are the internal and external stakeholders *of this part of the organization*? Describe how they are served as specifically as possible.	
3	How satisfied are internal and external customers *with this part of the organization*? What do they like most? Why? What do they like least? Why?	
4	How satisfied are the internal and external stakeholders with *this part of the organization*? What do they like most? What do they like least? Why?	
5	What do the customers and the stakeholders *of this part of the organization* believe is the major value added of this part of the organization? What value does the part add that could not be done faster, cheaper, or better than by others (such as external vendors or consultants)?	

Once this information has been collected and organized, it should be fed back to the organization's managers, leaders, and workers in ways that will capture their attention and alert them to what distinguishes the organization's products and services from those of others who might be regarded as competitors. What is especially good or bad about the company's products or services as assessed by customers and other stakeholders? How can the organization's core competencies be leveraged to achieve the most advantageous outcomes? How can the organization's weaknesses be addressed and their effects minimized?

Will a Cadre of Full-Time Workers Be Needed?

As noted in a previous part of this chapter, full-time workers may only be needed when they are absolutely essential for business reasons. For instance, it may take a long time to learn specifically what unique customers or other stakeholders need or expect. In addition, the organization's unique corporate culture may require that specific protocols be followed to achieve necessary results.

Many organizations, however, are exploring complex staffing arrangements rather than assuming that all—or even a majority of—workers will be so-called full-time, permanent staff. After all, a full-time staff can be expensive due to wages, salaries, benefits, and other costs of maintaining it, such as office space, equipment, tools, or other support resources. In many cases, however, organizational (and governmental) leaders still cling to traditional modes of thinking about how to staff for work. Or they may overuse some alternative approaches to staffing that they have had successful experience with, such as overtime, part-time workers, or temporary workers. Traditional ways of thinking could be challenged with many alternative approaches to staffing. The goal should always be to achieve work results (outcomes) in ways that meet or exceed customer or stakeholder requirements. How that is best done may be a focus of attention to drive down costs while maintaining or even increasing product or service quality.

How Many and What Kinds of Worker Talents/Outputs Will Be Needed?

If a cadre of full-time workers will be needed to achieve work results, how many and what kinds of people will really be needed? Will they actually perform the work or will some or all of them simply manage the work of others—such as vendors, consultants, part-time workers, temporary staff—to achieve the desired work results in products made or services delivered?

One way to make this determination is to examine the specific measurable work outputs of each organizational part. What products and/or services are absolutely essential for each functional area to provide so that the organization preserves its competitive advantage? Can the same (or even better) work results be achieved by means other than full-time workers? What is the added value of each functional area, and is it such that external providers could not supply the same or better work results at the same or lower cost?

Consider a simple example. One way an organization can manage its payroll is to do it all in-house. Full-time, permanent workers collect information and process the payroll, ensuring that everyone is paid on time. A second way to manage payroll is to outsource the entire process to a vendor. But in the latter case, someone may be needed inside the organization to interact with the vendor to ensure that the proper information is submitted so the payroll can be processed in a timely, efficient, and effective manner. A third way to manage payroll is to outsource everything, which will require the vendor to assume responsibility for seeking out any missing information from within the organization. Obviously, each approach to processing payroll may have advantages and disadvantages.

Can the Work Results Be Achieved with Alternative Staffing?

Staffing for work—and even for achieving the outputs of a specific job or task—need not be as simple as hiring a full-time worker. First, clarify exactly what needs to be done and how well. Make those characteristics of effective work measurable. Use a form like that appearing in Figure 4-5. First list the work duties or activities of the job. Then list the end products or services of

Figure 4-5: Clarifying What Needs to Be Done and How Well

Directions:	Use this worksheet to list all the work activities of a division, department, work group, or team. One way to do that is to write out all the work activities or duties from all the current job descriptions of the targeted group. Then indicate how the results of those activities can be measured according to quantity, quality, time, cost, or customer service. In the third column, indicate the targeted expectations and which results are most critical (key performance indicators) for the work to be done. Add paper if necessary.	
What Does the Group Do?	**How Are Results Measured?**	**What Are the Targeted Expectations for Results?**
1		
2		
3		
4		
5		

each duty or activity and what expectations exist for measuring the quality of that product or service as established by customers and/or other stakeholders. Finally, decide how to staff for accomplishing each activity or task.

Have Alternative Staffing Approaches Been Considered?

There is more than one way to achieve the results desired by customers or other stakeholders. Consider staffing strategies dominated by:

- *Who* does the work?
- *What* work do they do?
- *When* is the work done?
- *Where* is the work done?
- *Why* is the work done?
- *How* is the work done?
- *How much will it cost* to do the work?

Use the worksheet appearing in Figure 4-6 to brainstorm how to answer each question.

Figure 4-6: A Worksheet to Consider How to Get the Work Done

Directions: Once you have completed Exhibit 4.5, brainstorm on this worksheet about the most effective ways to achieve measurable work results. For each work result and activity listed in the left column, list ways to achieve that result in the right column. Consider (1) Who does the work or could do the work? (2) What work do they do or could do? (3) When is the work done or when could it be done? (4) Where is the work done or where could it be done? (5) Why is the work done or why could it be done? (6) How is the work done or could it be done? and (7) How much will it cost to do the work? Add paper if necessary.	
What Are the Desired Work Activities and Measurable Results?	**How Can the Work Be Done?**
1	
2	
3	
4	
5	
6	

The following subsections will treat each question in turn.

Who Does the Work? So-called who-based approaches to staffing focus on the number and kind of people needed to achieve the measurable work results to meet or exceed customer expectations. The workers may be full-time, permanent staff. But they could also be:

- Part-time permanent staff
- Part-time temporary staff
- External vendors
- External consultants
- Teams of workers who share the responsibility to achieve results
- Nontraditional workers such as retirees, older workers (past traditional retirement age), disadvantaged workers, displaced workers from other industries, disabled workers, students, interns, or others who do not match the profile of the traditional full-time permanent worker

Consider a simple example. Suppose that the work is very complicated to learn and requires a high level of professional knowledge. Take medical doctors, for instance. A hospital could rely on traditional staffing models. But an alternative would be to change who actually does parts of the work—such as nurse practitioners—who do some of the work of medical doctors. By subtracting some of the work from the medical staff and downloading it on a paraprofessional group, the organization's leaders can get the same or better quality and quantity of work results by relying on a different type of worker to do some of it.

What Work Do They Do? So-called what-based approaches to staffing will focus on changing the way work results are achieved so that what workers do can be adapted to the workers who are available to do it. Instead of "slotting workers in boxes on organization charts," the work is actually adapted to fit the people who are most readily available to do it.

Take a simple example. Suppose the work involves making change at the counter of a fast-food restaurant. Customers come in, order their food, and expect to leave with the food after they pay for it and receive their proper change. If the counter staff does not have good arithmetic skills—as is the case with many entry-level workers today in the United States—then the restaurant might engineer around the work by providing pictures of each product on the cash register. The counter staff simply punches in the order by selecting the pictures of the products ordered. The cash register then totals the cost of the order. The employee then enters how much money was provided, and the cash register indicates how much change is to be given to the customer. In effect, the way the work is done is changed to fit the skill sets of the workers available to do it.

When Is the Work Done? For some work results, timing does not matter so much. There may be ways to use time to your advantage by performing some or all of the work during "downtimes." Peak times may then be reserved for delivering the actual product or service.

Consider:

- Can the work be divided up and done at different times?
- Can time-consuming processes be spun off to be done by others, such as outsourcing agents or strategic allies?
- Can some work be done offshore or in other time zones?

Manufacturers, for instance, have long known about the value of suppliers who provide subassemblies. An automaker could take time out of the assembly line to build an automobile engine from scratch. But that would only slow the assembly line to a crawl, since it requires considerable time and effort to do that properly. Rather than rely on a station of the assembly line to do that, automakers may instead farm that work out to be done by others. Economies of scale can then be derived from suppliers of subassemblies who do part of the work. The same principle could be applied to many types of work.

Where Is the Work Done? In a global world, location does matter in getting the work done. Competitive wages and benefits are not the same worldwide. For instance, the average worker in Ethiopia lives on one U.S. dollar per day. While it is true that not everything can be done everywhere, it is possible to take advantage of different wage and benefit costs to do some things in some places and use the results in other places. That fact has been learned quite well by manufacturers in China and by information technology professionals in India. Even within the United States or other developed economies, wages and benefits are not the same across every location. Substantial savings may be realized by moving operations from a high-cost location, such as Manhattan or downtown Washington, D.C., to a lower-cost location such as Biloxi, Mississippi.

Why Is the Work Done? Work is not always done by individuals or organizations for the same reasons. Money is often a motivator. But it is not the only reason why people would work or why organizations would want to do work. Some individuals are excited by the mission of the organization and what it stands for. That is clear in dealing with charitable organizations like hospitals, the Red Cross, the Salvation Army, Goodwill, or UNICEF. Some individuals are excited by the intellectual challenges they may face in doing the work. It is often said that young engineers, for instance, are more willing to hire on with an organization and work to their peak when they are professionally challenged.

In short, why would an organization or an individual want to do the work and achieve the desired results? Will there be a marriage of interests that will put the person—or other organization—in a synergistic relationship that leads to a win for all concerned?

How Is the Work Done? Much attention has focused in recent years around process improvement and applications of technology to achieve desired results. Can the workflow be streamlined? Can technology change the work, or type of workers, needed to do the work? Is it possible to stop doing some work while doing more that will build on the competitive advantage of an organization?

How Much Will It Cost to Do the Work? Many staffing innovations are guided by a motivation to drive down the cost of full-time staff with full-time salaries, wages, and benefits. Correcting mistakes is often seen as the greatest cost and worthy of the most attention in driving down expenses, a key principle of lean manufacturing. But cost savings must always be regarded from the standpoint of how any change may affect customer satisfaction and perceptions about the quality received and the value of the work results.

Review Options Based on Advantages and Disadvantages

There is no such thing as a free lunch or free ride. Every workforce staffing option has advantages and disadvantages, including maintaining a full-time staff. Full-time workers are not always fully productive. And their benefit costs, particularly health insurance costs, can drive up workforce cost. That has prompted many employers to explore alternative staffing approaches.

Consider and Implement the Most Feasible Approaches

The organization's leaders should periodically take stock of the organization's strategic objectives and what makes the organization uniquely competitive in its industry or with its customers. Working backward from what results are to be achieved (products and/or services) and how they are to be measured to achieve customer satisfaction, the organization's leaders should then consider what kind of workforce is needed to best achieve the results. What percentage of the workforce should be full-time? What percentage of the workforce should be drawn from alternative staffing approaches?

Evaluate Results Over Time

Evaluating work and workforce planning is best done over time. Ways to measure it might include:

- Costs of wages and salaries compared to work outputs achieved
- Costs of wages and salaries compared to customer satisfaction achieved
- Costs of wages and salaries compared to market share achieved
- Costs of benefits compared to work outputs achieved
- Costs of benefits compared to customer satisfaction achieved
- Costs of benefits compared to market share achieved
- Percentage of full-time to part-time staff
- Turnover of full-time staff compared to turnover of other groups (temporary workers, etc.)

Some Options for Service Delivery or Product Manufacture

Figure 4-7 lists some common staffing approaches to getting work results. It lists some possible advantages and disadvantages of each approach. In many cases, employers may actually use a combination of approaches as one way to manage the risks of overusing one staffing approach. Review the list and add to the advantages and disadvantages.

(Text continues on page 102)

Figure 4-7: A List of Possible Ways to Staff for Getting Work Results

	Ways to Staff for Work Results	Advantage(s)	Disadvantage(s)
1	Recruit full-time staff from inside (job posting)	Workers can be trained over time to be better able to learn, meet, and exceed unique customer/stakeholder expectations; workers from inside know the corporate culture	Workers will be unaware of breakthrough efforts outside the organization; workers may be promoted as a reward for past performance rather than selected for their ability to meet challenges at higher levels of responsibility
2	Recruit full-time staff from outside	Workers can be trained over time to be better able to learn, meet and exceed unique customer/stakeholder expectations	Employer must pay for employee benefits, which will raise the cost of doing business
3	Develop full-time staff from inside (succession planning)	Promotion from within raises morale, improves engagement, and increases employee loyalty	Developing people costs time and money; employer incurs cost of employee benefits
4	Develop full-time staff from outside (establish partnerships with job-training programs or apprenticeship programs)	Employer can build talent to meet future needs at no cost or at low cost	Individuals not selected for employment will be public relations nightmares for the employer
5	Use overtime with full-time staff to address work peaks	Work can be accomplished with existing staff without incurring additional benefit costs	Overtime will increase costs and may stress out workers
6	Hire part-time staff to address periodic work peaks	Work can be accomplished without stressing out full-time workers and without incurring excessive overtime costs	Part-time workers have limited loyalty to the part-time employer and may not be adequately trained to do the work
7	Recruit virtual staff for full-time work	Virtual workers do not require offices or other equipment provided onsite	Virtual workers have limited loyalty to the employer and may be tough to reach if they do not want to be reached
8	Recruit virtual staff for part-time work	Same as above	Same as above
9	Recruit virtual staff for specific tasks	Cost is incurred only for work performed	Training and loyalty are limited
10	Recruit part-time workers from inside	Employees can meet demand where and when it exists	Employees may not have sufficient training and may have to worry about other work responsibilities in their home work location
11	Recruit part-time workers from outside	Part-time workers may not be eligible for the same benefits as full-time workers	Part-time workers may not be properly trained and may not be fully aware of customer/stakeholder expectations; they may not be loyal to the employer
12	Recruit flex-place workers	Workers can "float" to where they are needed	Workers may not be properly trained to meet expectations at all locations, and it may be too costly and time-consuming to train them

(continued)

Figure 4-7: (continued)

	Ways to Staff for Work Results	Advantage(s)	Disadvantage(s)
13	Promote from within	Workers know the corporate culture and should know customer/stakeholder expectations	Promotions may be rewards for past performance but not decided based on workers best able to meet the challenges at higher levels of responsibility
14	Outsource all the work	Cost savings may result; improved results may be obtained by those better able to provide those results	Total outsourcing means that the organization's leaders lose control of important processes and procedures and will be dependent on others for those
15	Outsource some of the work	Outsourcing allows the organization to focus on its core competency	Outsourcing means that the organization's leaders lose control of peripheral processes and procedures and may be dependent on others for those
16	Insource the work	Moving work domestically may improve service or product quality	Costs may increase; service or product quality may not increase as much as desired
17	Insource some of the work	Moving work domestically may improve service or product quality	Costs may increase service or product quality may not increase as much as desired
18	Automate the work	Automation reduces the possibility of human error and may increase productivity and quality	Automation can change the human interaction required to achieve results
19	Bid specific tasks or projects (places like elancer.com)	Cut costs; use the best talent	Accountability for results is not as great as with full-time workers
20	Have full-time teams do the work	Taps full creativity of a group and knocks down walls across job descriptions	A team does not necessarily have the ability to meet excessive work demands
21	Have part-time teams do the work (such as cross-functional task forces)	Allows some flexibility in tapping workers and expertise across functional areas	Workers will focus only on what they are held accountable for doing, and sometimes task force assignments are not tied to worker performance requirements
22	Redesign the organization so that work is reallocated	Old style box-and-line organization charts influence behaviors and may not be appropriate for getting best results in modern times	Reorganizations will not solve all problems
23	Redesign jobs so work is reallocated (trade duties/activities across jobs)	The work can be made more enriched and challenging to workers	Some workers do not want more enriched jobs unless they are paid for it
24	Improve/streamline the work process	Eliminates bottlenecks and inefficiencies in achieving work results	Has the tendency to focus only on the workflow without necessarilytaking customer/expectations into account
25	Form strategic alliances with other organizations to pool the work	Achieves economies of scale and can tie work to core competencies of different organizations; allows use of excess capacity	Different organizations may be appealing to different customers and stakeholders who have different needs

26	Form strategic alliances in the community to do the work	Achieves economies of scale in the community	Not all communities have all the skills needed to meet the needs of all organizations
27	Use free volunteers to do the work	Low cost	Limited commitment to organization because "you get what you pay for"; there may be no advantage to spending money to train free volunteers and so they may not know what they are doing
28	Form virtual alliances with other organizations to do the work	Can take advantage of excess time and capacity across organizations, allowing additional revenue sources	Limited commitment to the unique needs of specific groups of customers or stakeholders
29	Hire consultants from outside to do the work	Can get the best expertise to do the work; can gain advantages from knowledge gained across organizations	Can be expensive
30	Hire retirees on contract to do the work onsite	Retirees know the corporate culture and may require less training than new hires	Retirees may not respond well to authoritarian management practices
31	Hire retirees to do the work part-time or to fill in for others when out sick	Retirees know the corporate culture and may require less training than new hires	Retirees may not always be readily available to meet spur-of-the-moment needs
32	Hire retirees to do the work virtually	Retirees know the corporate culture and may require less training than new hires	Retirees may not be skilled in using the technology to do the work virtually; some people require social interaction to get best work results
33	Rethink the work process from scratch to reduce/change how much work is done or the skills needed to do the work	Rethinking the work may lead to breakthroughs in productivity	Can be costly and time-consuming to explore alternative approaches to achieving work results
34	Resequence how the work is done to save time	Rethinking work sequence may lead to ways to compress the work process	Resequencing may not always be useful
35	Have others do parts of the work (such as assemble subassemblies)	Can reduce the time it takes to get effective work results by outsourcing time-consuming or labor-intensive activities	Outsourcing agents may not always be aware of the unique needs of special customers or stakeholders
36	Have others do parts of the work and then have others assemble subassemblies	Can reduce the time it takes to get effective work results by outsourcing time-consuming or labor-intensive activities	Outsourcing agents may not always be aware of the unique needs of special customers or stakeholders
37	Hire temps or contingent workers to do the work	Lower benefit costs for temps or contingent workers	Temps and contingent workers may lack necessary training and their short-term relationship may not make it cost-effective to spend money on that

(continued)

Figure 4-7: (continued)

	Ways to Staff for Work Results	Advantage(s)	Disadvantage(s)
38	Shift duties across departments	Can achieve savings by shifting work to departments that are not as busy as others	Workers in other departments may not be familiar with the work or the unique needs of special internal or external customers and stakeholders
39	Shift tasks across jobs	Can take more advantage of existing workers and their skills	Workers may not have had the training to perform
40	Shift duties across organizations	Can achieve savings by shifting duties to other organizations	Workers in other organizations may not be familiar with the work or the unique needs of special internal or external customers and stakeholders
41	Have vendors do the work	Vendors may be willing to do the work because they want to secure a contract for other products or services	Vendors may not have adequate capabilities to meet the unique needs of the organization's customers and stakeholders
42	Have suppliers do the work	Suppliers may be willing to do the work because they want to secure a contract for other products or services	Suppliers may not have adequate capabilities to meet the unique needs of the organization's customers and stakeholders
43	Have distributors do the work	Distributors may be willing to do the work because they want to maintain a good relationship with their supplier	Distributors' workers may not have the necessary training to meet the unique needs of the organization's customers and stakeholders
44	Do only part of the work, but shift part of the work to consumers	Reduces cost	May lead consumers to look for other organizations that will not shift work to them
45	Focus only on what the organization does best and then outsource the rest	Allows the organization to focus on its core competency	The organization loses control of peripheral processes
46	Lease the workforce	Allows termination for cause without the usual concerns about wrongful discharge or discrimination/union complaints	May reduce commitment to the organization because another organization is the "real" employer
47	Lease specific jobs in the workforce	Allows termination for cause without the usual concerns about wrongful discharge or discrimination/union complaints	May reduce commitment to the organization because another organization is the "real" employer
48	Cross-train workforce (airline gate agents can help load luggage if necessary)	Allows workers prepared to fill in during peak times or when others are out sick or on vacation	May lead to union grievances in unionized workers unless workers are paid for doing extra or different work
49	Employ family members at low rates	Builds family commitment to the employer	May lead to problems of nepotism

50	Employ student interns from high school, college, or graduate school	Reduce cost; give students experience	Students may lack experience; students may not have proper training or commitment to the employer
51	Employ summer workers to do work	Lower cost; may give a chance to try out possible workers	Workers may not have adequate training and may not be fully committed to the organization
52	Employ workers during specific peak seasons (such as Christmas workers for retailers)	Lower cost; may give a chance to try out possible workers	Workers may not have adequate training and may not be fully committed to the organization
53	Employ special groups of workers (such as displaced workers, displaced housewives, veterans, or other special groups)	Provides opportunity for good public relations may yield special benefits if customers or stakeholders are from the same group as the one employed	Workers may require special management approaches, and managers may need to be trained to meet the special challenges posed by a unique type of worker
54	Combine any or all of the methods above to achieve measurable work results to meet or exceed customer/stakeholder expectations	Achieve the benefits of several approaches, including balancing lower costs with other benefits	May require more complicated management skills from supervisors, managers, and executives

Note that everything up to this point has focused on the strategic level, that is, how an organization can achieve measurable results, tied to leveraging its core competency over time. But it is also possible to do that tactically by considering how to get the work done best for a team or even for a specific job as vacancies occur. See Figures 4-8 and 4-9 for worksheets to use in considering tactical staffing issues.

How to Close Staffing Gaps

It is sometimes said that there are only two ways to close staffing gaps. One way is to promote from within. The other way is to hire from outside.

However, as the previous section of this chapter has demonstrated, that is not always true. There are indeed other options for staffing. *The work results must be managed before the workforce is to be planned or managed.* And work can be managed if it is:

- Eliminated
- Streamlined
- Outsourced
- Insourced
- Reengineered (changing how the work is processed—the throughput)
- Offshored
- Reorganized (the organization changes how responsibility for work outputs is allocated to departments and jobs)

One general rule of thumb is that the organization should never lose control of the essence of whatever makes it uniquely competitive (that is, its *core competency*). That means that anything related to the core competency should never be outsourced or handed over to those without the talents to do it in ways uniquely suited to the organization's customers or stakeholders.

Once it is clear what work will be done and what results are desired, then the organization's leaders are best able to staff for that work. They can do that by managing who does the work, what work they do, when they do the work, where they do the work, why they do the work, how they do the work, and how much it costs to maintain various staffing groups.

(Text continued on page 107)

Figure 4-8: A Worksheet for Optimizing the Results of a Work Team

Directions: Use this worksheet to consider the various ways by which to get the work of an entire job team done. Do not assume that every job currently performed on the team has to be filled. Instead, begin by listing the work activities of al jobs on the team to be performed under column 1 below. (If you have trouble doing that, go to the online version of *The Dictionary of Occupational Titles*, look up the job title, and list activities provided in the left column.) Then, under column 2, indicate the most important activities of the entire team, that is, the key performance indicators for the team. That should result in only three to five most important activities. Then, under column 3, indicate how to measure those key performance indicators for the team using metrics linked to quantity, quality, time, cost, or customer service. Then, under column 4, list all the ways that each key work activity could be accomplished without hiring a replacement on the team to do the job. Consider such options as eliminating the work entirely, outsourcing it, using overtime trading it to other workers on the team or other parts of the organization, having the work performed by a temporary or contingent worker, or any other creative approach you can think of. Under column 5, list any advantages or disadvantages from the alternatives you proposed and consider the costs and benefits of the alternatives. Finally, describe under column 6 how the work will be done according to the metrics pinpointed under column 3. Add paper as necessary.

Column 1	Column 2	Column 3	Column 4	Column 5	Column 6
Work activities of the team	Which work activities are key performance indicators? (Check three to five)	How can the key performance indicators be measured by outputs?	What are some ways to achieve the measurable key performance indicators without hiring a full-time worker for the team?	What are the advantages and disadvantages of each way to achieve the key performance indicators listed under column 4?	How can the work best be accomplished and results achieved?
1					
2					
3					

(continued)

Figure 4-8: (continued)

Column 1	Column 2	Column 3	Column 4	Column 5	Column 6
Work activities of the team	Which work activities are key performance indicators? (Check three to five)	How can the key performance indicators be measured by outputs?	What are some ways to achieve the measurable key performance indicators without hiring a full-time worker for the team?	What are the advantages and disadvantages of each way to achieve the key performance indicators listed under column 4?	How can the work best be accomplished and results achieved?
4					
5					
6					
7					
8					

Figure 4-9: A Worksheet for Filling a Job Vacancy

Directions: Use this worksheet to consider the various ways by which to get the work done. Do not assume that every job has to be filled. Instead, begin by listing the work activities to be performed under column 1 below. (If you have trouble doing that, go to the online version of *The Dictionary of Occupational Titles*, look up the job title, and list activities provided in the left column.) Then, under column 2, indicate the most important activities, that is, the key performance indicators for the job. That should result in only three to five most important activities. Then, under column 3, indicate how to measure those key performance indicators using metrics linked to quantity, quality, time, cost, or customer service. Then, under column 4, list all the ways that each key work activity could be accomplished without hiring a replacement to do the job. Consider such options as eliminating the work entirely, outsourcing it, trading it to other workers or other parts of the organization, offshoring it, using overtime, having the work performed by a temporary or contingent worker, or any other creative approach you can think of. Under column 5, list any advantages or disadvantages from the alternatives you proposed and consider the costs and benefits of the alternatives. Finally, describe under column 6 how the work will be done according to the metrics pinpointed under column 3. Add paper as necessary.

Column 1	Column 2	Column 3	Column 4	Column 5	Column 6
Work activity	Which work activities are key performance indicators? (Check three to five)	How can the key performance indicators be measured by outputs?	What are some ways to achieve the measurable key performance indicators without hiring a full-time worker?	What are the advantages and disadvantages of each way to achieve the key performance indicators listed under column 4?	How can the work best be accomplished and results achieved?
1					
2					
3					

(continued)

Figure 4-9: (continued)

Column 1 Work activity	Column 2 Which work activities are key performance indicators? (Check three to five)	Column 3 How can the key performance indicators be measured by outputs?	Column 4 What are some ways to achieve the measurable key performance indicators without hiring a full-time worker?	Column 5 What are the advantages and disadvantages of each way to achieve the key performance indicators listed under column 4?	Column 6 How can the work best be accomplished and results achieved?
4					
5					
6					
7					
8					

Select Staffing Approaches to Align Talent to Organizational Objectives

Many managers complain that it is nearly impossible to get rid of poor performers. It is a complaint heard globally. Often the HR department is blamed because managers who experience behavioral or performance problems with workers find they must use progressive corrective action systems. That means they must apply due process by giving workers an oral warning, a written warning, and sometimes a suspension. Only after workers are given ample opportunities to improve can they be terminated.

While it seems that this approach is equitable and fair by giving workers the chance to improve before they are terminated for cause, the reality is that applying such approaches is fraught with problems. Managers may find that they must defend themselves against predictable defenses raised by workers. For instance, workers may claim that their supervisor does not like them. They may also claim that they were not trained, informed of the requirements or expectations ahead of time, or treated the same way as other workers. Workers may also appeal to their coworkers for support, which places managers in a tenuous position—especially when U.S. employee privacy laws may make it difficult or impossible for managers to explain to other workers why a worker was treated as he or she was treated.

These problems with managing full-time workers can make it appealing for employers to explore alternative staffing options. If all workers are leased (work for a middleman employer between the organization and workers), are temporary workers (hired by the day or on short-term contracts), are retirees (who work for supplementary income), are consultants (who also work on contract), are outsourced (so that workforce management becomes an issue for contractors), or are employed in other creative ways, the employer may incur less cost while receiving better results—and may maintain the ability to "let people go" easier than a painful termination for cause or downsizing initiative.

Frequently Asked Questions

Whenever staffing optimization is raised, employers may have some predictable questions. A few of those are posed—and answered—below.

Question 1: Where could an organization's leaders start in optimizing staff?

Answer: Start with the end results in mind. Clarify the targets, such as the ideal profile of the products to be made and/or the services to be offered. Find ways to test management assumptions against customer/stakeholder needs, wants, preferences, and expectations. Then work backward from the measurable end results to discover the most efficient and effective ways to achieve those results. Do not make assumptions about what is best; rather, experiment with different approaches. Do some scenario planning to see what approaches might end up costing less but yielding the same or better results than traditional approaches, such as staffing with full-time workers.

Question 2: Will staff optimization lead to more complexity for managers?

Answer: Yes, it will. Hiring traditional full-time workers makes it easier to control who shows up for work on time, and it is easier to see who looks busy at their desks. But newer approaches to staffing will require new approaches to management in which workers are objectively measured for the quality and quantity of results they achieve. It will not be as easy as policing people who are late for work because teleworkers may not show up physically. When they are absent virtually, it may be more difficult to determine why they are not online.

Question 3: Optimizing staff may sound scary to workers who are accustomed to traditional, full-time employment. How can that fear be addressed?

Answer: People who are accustomed to full-time employment may find a new approach to optimizing staffing quite unsettling. They may not know who will pay their benefits—and, indeed, more individuals may end up having to pay for benefits themselves if they work virtually and part-time for many employers. Highly productive people will see their take-home salaries increase dramatically because they will get more work referrals. They will be less often victimized by managers who could conceal their talents for fear that they cannot replace good people when organizations are downsizing. But workers will have to be more entrepreneurial. They will have to do a better job of career planning, thinking ahead about how each assignment they accept may affect their future work prospects.

Question 4: Is downsizing itself a way to optimize staffing?

Answer: It can be. But that is not to say it always is. If the same (or more) work of the same (or greater) quality can be done with fewer people and/or at less cost, then downsizing can lead to staff optimization. But great care should be taken in deciding *who* should be downsized and *how* their work results will be achieved after they leave. Unfortunately, many employers cut heads first and then later worry about work reallocation. That leads to important work "falling through the cracks" and stressed-out high potentials, who may conclude that they would be better off working somewhere else.

Question 5: What are the most common mistakes made when an employer embarks on an effort to optimize staffing?

Answer: The most common mistake is not considering a range of alternatives before first seizing on one and implementing it. There is a decided tendency to "fire, ready, and aim" when trying to cut costs while sustaining or increasing the quality and quantity of work results. A second common mistake is to forget that continual communication is needed. Managers tend to make one announcement about a change and expect everyone to understand. They do not. Continuing communication is needed. A third common mistake is to assume that staff optimization always requires a "top-down" approach. But it may not. Workers can be involved in the process of identifying the desired end results/targets, making those targets measurable, and pinpointing the best ways to achieve them.

Chapter Summary

This chapter described approaches to optimizing staffing. In a bid to cut costs, many employers are experimenting with innovative approaches to achieving quality work results with alternatives to traditional full-time employment. This chapter introduced a model to guide thinking through these alternatives in a systematic way. The chapter offered a range of possible options to staff for effective and efficient service delivery or product making. It also pointed to the most common advantages and disadvantages of each option.

CHAPTER 5

OPTIMIZE THE FUTURE WORK AND WORKFORCE

THIS CHAPTER DISCUSSES how to define and document an organization's future state to optimize future work and workforce. Specifically, the chapter addresses how to review existing future state assessments and organizational objectives; optimize future objectives; define work required to deliver those objectives; scan future trends that affect future work and worker results; determine critical functions/processes/roles for the future state; consider alternative workforce approaches; look at the future state organization; conduct value-for-money analysis; integrate objectives, work, and talent management; and conduct financial analysis.

Review Existing Future State Assessments and Organizational Objectives

Before discussing the mechanics of assessing and documenting the future state position of an organization, let's reflect on the rationale and value for doing so.

In most cases, there is typically a trigger event for an organization's leaders to look beyond the present business plan or next year's budget to the creation of a future state plan and/or to review an existing plan. In chapter 2, example 2-5, we discussed the case of Firm X's diminishing success in sales. You may remember that Firm X's leaders needed to reinvent the organization because it was being outmaneuvered by its competitors in engineering, manufacturing, and sales. The opposite—increases in sales and demand—can also be a likely trigger point since such increases typically create pressure on the organization's ability to deliver products or services. The dangerous time for many organizations, however, is when they are performing adequately relative to forecasts. In such situations there appears to be no real imperative to plan beyond the next forecast or budget period. All is perceived to be going well. Because of an organization's current success, the organization's leaders are satisfied to continue their present practices. But if they fail to pay attention to the future state, the organization will likely be surprised by market events and/or demands in the same way Firm X drifted into a major problem. The risk of ignoring the future, because current performance is adequate, is a constant and significant danger for all organizations. Hence, there needs to be a continuously renewed link from the future state, or where the leaders want to be by a certain time, back to the current state, or where they are today. But it is very easy for an organization's leaders to fall into an "activity trap" where no real focus is placed on outcomes and objectives beyond tomorrow's budget or perspective.

An *activity trap* is best described as the focus on process and activity, not on outcome, when the outcome is the continuing success of the organization. As a powerful example of the potential to drift into a major problem, think of the impact on photographic film manufacturers and distributors with the change to digital photography. Fortunes had been made through the processing and manufacture of photographic film. The industry was extremely profitable; companies were meeting their targets in sales and profitability. What would have happened if these companies had only focused on the near term with no regard for the changing demands of the future state imposed by the new photographic technology?

While engaged in their current activity, decision makers leading industries and companies need to constantly review what they are doing in terms of their future position, that is, to consider the future state. What is the objective and what needs to be done to achieve it? If attention is only on the near term, the opportunity to determine a clear path to the future is extremely limited. Yet common cries from business leaders are, "How can we plan for five years out when we do not know for sure what the next quarter will bring?" or "All of our focus is on quarterly earnings and semiannual results. Trying to align these with a five-year plan is impossible!" and, finally, "Technology and demand are changing so fast we do not know what the company will look like in twelve months!"

These statements share a common theme: The focus is on short-term objectives. Indeed, it could be argued that this focus has been one key contributor to the economic pressure and challenges the world has been facing in the second decade of the twenty-first century. If an organization's focus includes the future state, however, decisions will be much easier to make and the path toward the future state will be much clearer. But if the focus is only on the near term (for example, the market cap/share price this quarter), the potential to fall into the activity trap is a real and constant threat.

Another important point is that the length of the plan depends on the organization and the objective. The notion that fast-paced environments preclude long-range planning is quite misleading. The length in calendar periods is not as important as the actual plan. For example, in some industries a two-year plan is seen as adequate while in others a fifteen-year plan is essential.

A well-managed plan impacts organizational performance, profitability, engagement, cost control, and focus. If these aren't important to a particular organization, then perhaps a future state position and a set of clear objectives aren't necessary. However, the results of this stance may be unexpected and detrimental to the well-being of the organization.

Define and Document the Future State

Business plans are often projections based on current activity and history. But a future state document begins with the premise of a zero base as described in chapter 2. To begin to build toward a future state position and optimize future work and staffing, we should ask this important question: *"What would you expect to see in a well-constructed future state positioning document?"* This foundational question was included in the HR performance audit process described in chapter 2. A high-level view of a well-constructed future state positioning document forms the blueprint for a future state plan. Once leadership has decided to support a future state review, a project team needs to be established. The project team should determine if the members collectively have the necessary internal skills to successfully complete the project. One key to the successful development of a future state document is team facilitation. It would be remarkable for one person in any large organization to have the depth of knowledge and broad-ranging expertise to create an optimal result for a future state plan. In fact, it is often beneficial for the lead facilitator not to have any in-depth knowledge of the organization's business. Asking "dumb questions" can often elicit interesting answers, some of which may eventually be proven to be based on false assumptions. As with any significant undertaking, it is imperative that an activity of this nature have sponsors who have the necessary authority to support it. See Figure 5-1.

Figure 5-1: Template for Lean but Agile Confirmation of Objectives

Estimated Total Days: XX

Pre-Workshop Interview	
Steps	– Coordinate meetings with CEO, key functional managers, and internal auditors and walk through with HR – Send out interview "road map" prior to each interview, to allow for preparation – Meet with the CEO and file findings – Meet with key functional managers and file findings – Meet with internal auditors and file findings – Walk through with HR and file findings – E-mail follow-up to interviewees to thank for time
Who is involved	Project team member(s) Lead facilitator Senior HR auditor (if applicable) CEO Key functional managers Internal auditors (if applicable) Human resources
Expected time frames	CEO—1.5 hours Other interviews—30 minutes each

Expected outcomes	– *From meeting with CEO:*
	  • "View from the Top"
	  • Develop project team's understanding of the CEO's expectations
	  • Develop project team's understanding of the organization, its corporate vision, and organizational goals before the workshop
	  • Confirm the key functional managers to be interviewed
	  • Establish workshop time frames
	  • Arrange follow-up meeting date
	– *From meeting with execs:*
	  • Understanding of the project's information needs
	  • Data gathering: business plans, formal spans of control and project plans for each of the organizational goals
	  • Establish any evidence of goal linkage to the organization's talent-management system
	– *From meeting with auditors*
	  • Understanding of approach
	  • Knowledge of where to obtain particular information, and from whom
	– *Walk-through with HR*
	  • Review of the HRIS/TM documentation, processes and systems, how current, comprehensive

Costs, cost management	– Materials – Room rent – Project team members conducting interviews – Cost management, keep appointments
Assumptions	*Number of key functional managers (interviewees)—determine by size and available time*
Tool kit	– Interview pack—include pre-interview "road map" – CEO checklist – Functional management checklist – Internal auditors checklist – HR checklist – Feedback report template (corporate goals and linkage to human capital)

(continued)

Figure 5-1: (continued)

Review/document corporate objectives and linkages to human capital	
Steps	— Compile interview data — Compose report for presentation to CEO — Meet with CEO to deliver report and present findings — Discuss likely participants for and timings of Best Practices Workshop
Who is involved	Project team Auditor Admin CEO
Expected time frames	1 day off-site 30-min. presentation with CEO
Expected outcomes	Report/presentation to CEO detailing findings
Costs, cost management	Materials
Assumptions	
Tool kit	Report template
Best Practices Workshop—Creating executive line of sight to the objective	
Steps	— Coordinate date that all nominated attendees can attend — Book full-day workshop following all interviews — Book meeting room and invite all participants — Organize lunch and materials — Send out prework pack — Following the meeting . . . participant at next meeting and "go to" person going forward
Who is involved	Project team Lead facilitator Senior consultant HR auditor Admin Senior executives—optimum number is 10—may not necessarily include all of the senior management team or those interviewed initially
Expected time frames	Full day
Expected outcomes	— Personal introductions—building relationships — Understand the participant expectations for the workshop and project — Clarification of the project objectives and expectations of delivery — Feedback findings to participants — Confirmation and understanding of the organization's vision—vision lock — Unpack vision into goals and objectives — Participants for following meeting and "go to" person going forward (follow up to the meeting)
Costs, cost management	— Lunch — Materials — Room rent
Assumptions	
Tool kit	— Participant workbook—including workshop objectives — Agenda — What should participants prepare and bring — Template of workshop data — Follow up e-mail?

Figure 5-1: (continued)

Interview Executives	
Steps	— Walk through
Who is involved	Project team Auditor Senior consultant Admin Executives decided by senior executives following the Best Practices Workshop.
Expected time frames	30 min. per interview
Expected outcomes	— Understanding of the project's information needs — Data gathering—business plans, formal spans of control and project plans for each of the organizational goals — Establish any evidence of goal linkage to the organization's talent-management system
Costs, cost management	
Assumptions	
Tool kit	— Interview pack—include pre-interview "road map"
Workshop linkage of objectives and future direction to HCM requirements	

Steps	— Design matrix
	— Decide on outcomes
	— Decide what the outputs are to achieve the outcomes
	— Integrate outcomes and outputs into matrix
	  • One worksheet per outcome
	  • One output per line item
	  • Populate matrix column headings with the organization's departments or key functions or units (e.g., marketing, warehousing, IT, call center)
	  • Populate cells with the appropriate forum and contributions to determine the impact of that output on each listed department (function or unit)
	  • Apply weighting scores to each impact according to its criticality in influencing the output
	— Facilitate management discussion to list the impacts in relative priority order
	— Attribute responsibility for managing those impacts, and derive KPIs for particular managers and teams
	— Complement with a risk-return analysis to facilitate the development of a priority action plan
	— Unpack impacts into human capital requirements to understand associated talent implications and requisite competencies for each
	— Identify go-to people for the remainder of the project—key managers to coordinate information, access, or people for project team

Who is involved	Project team Lead facilitator Auditor Senior consultant Admin Executives decided by senior executives following the Best Practices Workshop
Expected time frames	— Half-day preparation — 1 full-day workshop
Expected outcomes	— Matrix highlighting outputs and outcomes, and their impacts on the organization, to determine the human capital requirements — Identification of key contacts — Establish date and attendees of next meeting
Costs, cost management	— Room booking — Materials — Sustenance
Assumptions	Maximum 30 goals/linkages
Tool kit	— Participant workbook, including what should participants prepare and bring — Agenda — List of workshop objectives — Matrix — Project coordination of each slice of the organization to facilitate whole-of-organization consistency

A template of a project initiation meeting can be seen in Figure 5-2.

The following fourteen key elements are essential for creating or reviewing a plan to optimize the future work and workforce:

1. A Defined Timeline Beyond the Current Budgeting Focus

Typically, this is a five-year-plus plan. As mentioned previously, length in terms of time is not the important factor. This review exercise is about setting objectives beyond the current, easily foreseen forecast of the organization. The future state position timeline is set based on direction from senior leaders or the corporate board.

2. Clear, Concise Organizational Future Objectives

Aspirational goals are not objectives. The overall organizational objective needs to be established, providing guidance on products and/or services to be delivered, target markets, and locations. The future state definitions document should include a high-level description of the future state business activities. This would include products and services offered, target markets, organization locations, size of operations, activities undertaken, and target profitability. An effective way to do that is to host a series of facilitated workshops with senior leaders to ensure that the vision and objectives are clearly documented, linked, and understood by all stakeholders.

3. Optimization of Future Objectives

As has been mentioned, the concepts of *lean work* and a *lean workforce* are based on continually realigning the definition and delivery of the human capital required to deliver organizational objectives. Reviewing these objectives in light of where the organization stands on the path to the future state allows for both the objectives and the strategy to be reevaluated. Current workforce-management and talent-management technologies allow leaders to gain a real-time snapshot of how the organization is tracking against its objectives. A formal review conducted on a six-month cycle is also recommended. This is typically achieved in a workshop environment where the vision (what the organization wants to become) is confirmed, understood, and agreed on by all by asking:

- Is the vision current?
- Is it the agreed-on vision?

Figure 5-2: Agenda-Project Initiation Meeting

Date:

Location:

Estimated Time	Discussion Point	Notes
	Icebreaker	
	Introductions	
	Expectations	
	Project Plan	
	Run through Lean but Agile proposed program	
	Overall stages	
	Optimum outcome	
	Stage One	
	Detailed review	
	Align stage one approach to organizational requirements	
	Define stage one project timelines, list of key stakeholders, targeted interview outcomes, and interviewees	
	Formalize project team, responsibilities, and deliverables	
	Agree on communication and change management strategy	
	Governance	
	Key contacts and sponsors	
	Issue escalation/resolution	
	Maintaining the plan	
	Communication model (how often, by what means, meeting organizer/chair)	
	Invoicing Process	

- Is it realistic?

- Is it based on evidence and research?

The vision is the foundation for achieving the long-term objectives. The strategic drivers for realizing the vision and each objective are assessed for achievability, taking into account the current state of factors as determined by the environmental scan suggested in chapter 2.

4. Evidence That the Objectives Are Achievable

Evidence of the ability of the organization to deliver on each objective is critical. Leadership must understand the basis for this objective and the likelihood it can be met. Examples of evidence may take such forms as market research, research and development plans, manufacturing confirmations, client demand assessments, surveys, and competitor analysis. This assessment exercise is typically a follow-up requirement of the first facilitated meeting.

5. The Criteria for the Evidence and, in Turn, the Achievability

Once the objectives are established with verifiable evidence, the criteria used to establish them form the basis for the ongoing assessment of future achievability. For instance, one criterion for a particular targeted growth may be the global economy's continuing growth beyond X percent per annum. If monitored, a fall below X percent would prove a valuable indicator of potential problems in achieving the objective.

6. An Analysis, a Definition, and a Description of the Work Required to Deliver These Objectives

The work requirement may change due to many factors, including (1) a change in corporate direction (for example, Nike moving from being a manufacturer to a marketer), or (2) a change in business focus or products (for example, Kodak ceasing photographic film processing). These are just two examples. But the important outcome for this analysis is an in-depth understanding of what work is required to deliver the desired objectives. This analysis is best gathered and aggregated through workshops or retreats with appropriate subject matter experts.

7. A Scan of Future Trends That Affect Future Work and Worker Results

We have seen massive changes in business globally in the past few decades. For instance, in the past twenty years alone there has been a marked improvement in technology and all forms of communications, thus improving information availability and access. This instant access to information has created enormous opportunities for new products and services. But it has also changed the way some individuals prefer to work. Many organizations are decentralized, with employees working remotely rather than from a central location.

While these improvements and changes are positive, there are, however, many potential issues facing organizations in the twenty-first century, including:

- An aging population
- The reduction in the available workforce
- The trend for decentralized labor delivery
- Emerging labor markets
- Environmental considerations
- The global economy
- The local economy
- The availability of funds
- The cost of labor

For every negative issue, though, there seem to be abundant opportunities as well. For instance, the needs of an aging population are creating a broad cross-section of new business opportunities in the leisure and health-care industries. The focus on caring for the environment has also created opportunities for developing and marketing renewable energy.

When leaders have a detailed understanding of their organizational objectives, they can more effectively adapt to any changes in criteria for achieving these objectives. Yet it is increasingly important that organizations focus on the key criteria that impact the delivery of desired objectives.

8. A Value-for-Money Analysis

If an activity is to be defined as *value for money*, it means that it must be effective, economical, and efficient (the three E's). Once the work requirement and the functional requirements are determined, a high-level scan of the capability of the organization and workforce to deliver value for money is prudent.

For instance, assume that an organization has determined that its future state would involve manufacturing a product that requires a high labor component. Would it not be prudent to demonstrate to leadership the ability of this function to deliver value for money as soon as possible? The leaders at Firm X in the example in chapter 2 had not reviewed the value-for-money criterion for their manufacturing operations, so their future plans were based on the premise that they could compete with other companies with their product. That mistake nearly caused a complete failure of Firm X's business. This analysis required the combined efforts of the project team, leadership, and finance to analyze the value for money delivered by each of the proposed work requirements. The HR audit process (see appendix) described in chapter 2 can assist in determining a defensible, rigorous outcome from this analysis.

9. Determination of Critical Functions/Processes/Roles for the Future State

Once the work requirement is clearly defined, a review of the functions needed to deliver the work should be well-documented and supported with relevant analysis and process requirements. There should be evidence of an analysis of what is functionally critical to deliver the work. The issue of criticality is covered extensively in chapter 2.

In turn, a well-documented and evidenced high-level workforce plan describing the critical roles and capabilities required within each function is expected. The details of how to analyze these roles and determine optimum capability requirements is documented in chapter 3. This analysis involves subject matter experts, leadership, human resources, and the project team.

10. The Future State Organizational Structure

An organizational model demonstrating the key elements and structure—including the management structure, divisional structure, products and services, anticipated locations, and reporting framework—would also be expected. Again the leadership group and project team need to be involved in establishing an effective organizational design. Much experimentation has been taking place in many organizations in recent years to rethink the traditional box-and-line depictions of organizational charts, which can be detrimental if they shape behaviors in unproductive ways.

11. Consideration of Alternative Workforce Approaches

Chapter 4 gives a detailed review of alternative workforce approaches. The key consideration in determining the appropriate staffing approach should be value for money.

12. Decision to Build, Buy, or Outsource

The decision to build talent, bring the talent in, or simply outsource the particular function should be driven by a range of factors that include:

- The criticality of the role
- The current and future availability of resources
- Value-for-money considerations
- Quality and availability of outsource partners

13. Integration of Organizational Objectives, Work, and Talent Management

To optimize the workforce, a similar framework of definition, assessment, and talent pool optimization, as discussed in chapter 3, is required. Indeed, the only additional step is to define the capability level of the roles required at the nominated future point.

However, to optimize future work and the workforce, there needs to be tight integration of the organizational objectives and talent management. This requires building a framework that includes organizational objectives and work analysis.

Chapter 3 describes a well-founded, traditional talent-management process. But if talent management is to be integrated seamlessly into the delivery of organizational objectives, you need the drivers of talent management to be work and organizational objectives. This is best illustrated by Figure 5-3.

This approach will give the talent-management framework slightly more complexity. When we begin and conclude with organizational objectives as part of a continuous process, we also need some level of review and realignment. A graphical representation of an organizational objective focused and optimized in the talent-management model can be seen in Figure 5-4.

14. Detailed Financial Analysis

A detailed financial analysis of the future state position must align with the organizational objectives in terms that emphasize how the objectives will be supported by the financial model proposed. In commercial organizations, objectives may be reflected in market capitalization, shareholder returns,

Figure 5-3: Optimized Talent-Management Framework

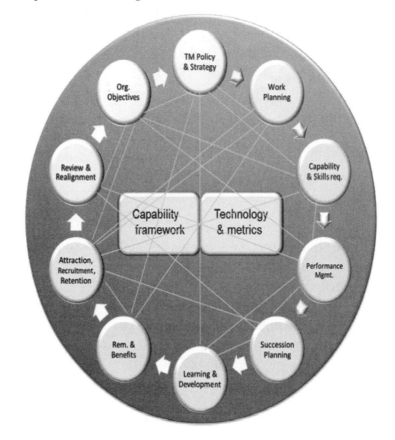

Figure 5-4: Linking Organizational Objectives to Talent Management

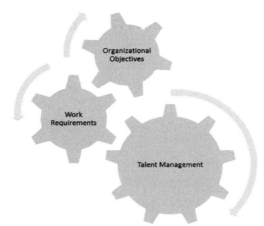

revenue, and/or profit targets. In public sector and not-for-profit organizations the linkage may be service provision, dollars spent per constituent, and similar metrics. This task sits firmly with finance, with project team support as required.

By reviewing your future position utilizing the fourteen key elements we have discussed, you will be continually aligning your organization's work and workforce to deliver the organizational objective. This process of continual alignment and the utilization of work and workforce methodologies and strategies discussed in this book will create the perfect foundation for a Lean but Agile organization. Additional tools for getting this process started can be found in Figures 5-5, 5-6, and 5-7. Use them to interview decision makers.

Chapter Summary

This chapter discussed how to document an organization's future state to optimize future work and workforce. The chapter addressed how to review existing future state assessments and organizational objectives; optimize future objectives; define work required to deliver those objectives; scan future trends that affect future work and worker results; determine critical functions/processes/roles for the future state; consider alternative workforce approaches; look at the future state organization; conduct value-for-money analysis; integrate objectives, work, and talent management; and conduct financial analysis.

Figure 5-5: Checklist for Discussion with the CEO

Date:	✓	Note/Working paper
Organizational performance. Consider operating results, profit, markets. Obtain recent annual reports.		
Obtain a copy of the organization's structure.		
Number of employees.		
Locations; products and services.		
Business plans for the organization, and its respective parts.		
Strengths.		
Weaknesses.		
Opportunities.		
Market/competitor activity.		
Challenges.		
Key risks.		
Vision/key objective/What's on the radar?		
Are there project plans for each of the objectives, to demonstrate the pathways, milestones, roles, and responsibilities for the achievement of those goals? In other words, are they SMART objectives: Specific, Measurable, Achievable, Realistic, and Time-based Are they evidenced?		
Are these objectives linked to the organization's talent management system, with implications for recruitment, training and development, organization structure? Is this evidenced?		
Confirm the key functional managers to be interviewed before the workshop(s).		

Figure 5-6: Checklist for Stage 1 Discussion with Functional Managers

Date: Manager:	✓	Note/Working paper
Obtain copy of their formal span of control/the structure of their area of responsibility.		
Number of employees.		
Locations; products and services.		
Business plans for their part of the organization.		
Are the organizational goals understood?		
Are they agreed?		
Are there project plans for each of the goals, to demonstrate the pathways, milestones, roles, and responsibilities for the achievement of those goals? In other words, are they SMART objectives: Specific, Measurable, Achievable, Realistic, and Time-based? Are they evidenced?		
Are these objectives linked to the organization's talent-management system, with implications for recruitment, training and development, organization structure? Is this evidenced?		
Challenges		
Are there any other thoughts about the project and/or the process?		

Figure 5-7: Manager Preparation for the Workshop(s)

You will be asked to briefly outline:

1. Your area of responsibility within the organization.
2. Your expectations for the workshop and the project.

Please be prepared for discussion around the following points:

3. The organization's vision (what the organization wants to become) is confirmed, understood, and agreed by all.
   a. Is the vision current?
   b. Is it the agreed vision?
   c. Is it realistic?
   d. Is it based on evidence and research?

4. Then the vision will be unpacked into goals and objectives as the strategic drivers for achieving the vision. The strategic plan sets the stage for creating the HR plans and competencies for delivering on these strategies and meeting any identified challenges. Starting with the strategic vision and goals (the outcomes; some call them the strategic priorities), we will ask the question: *What do we have to do to achieve those outcomes?* In other words, *What are the outputs to achieve those outcomes?*

5. How, and to what extent, will the output impact, for example, systems, structure, services to be provided, infrastructure, HR, payroll, IT, buildings and amenities, property acquisition, and finance?

6. Where are the most significant impacts, and in which functions and units?

7. List the impacts in relative priority order.

8. Unpack each impact into human capital requirements; that is, *What are the associated talent implications/requisite competencies for each impact?*

9. Then, *strategic* and *key* roles for the future are identified to determine:
   - What are the *strategic* roles critical to all business strategies and long-term growth? These are critical to driving long-term competitive advantage, with specialized skills or knowledge.
   - What are the *key* roles that are critical to some business strategies? These are core to delivering on the organization's products and/or services.

Project Team expectations:
   - You will contribute your opinions.
   - Diversity of opinions is valued and respected.
   - All ideas and points of view have value.
   - Honor time. We have an ambitious agenda.
   - Cell phone courtesy. You all have demanding responsibilities outside this workshop. We ask that these responsibilities be left at the door. Your attention is needed for the full meeting. Please turn cell phones, or any other communication item with an on/off switch, to "silent."

CHAPTER 6

MANAGE AND MAINTAIN A LEAN BUT AGILE WORKFORCE

WHAT DOES A LEAN BUT AGILE ORGANIZATION look like? At one extreme, a few organizations are beginning to morph into loosely affiliated, sometimes far-flung networks of contractors that readily increase and decrease as work demand varies. Organizations like these bear little resemblance to traditional organizations (see Case Study 1: Acme Consulting). But in most cases, Lean but Agile organizations do not look strikingly different from most other companies. They work progressively and systematically, though, at becoming more Lean but Agile, and in the process they are making significant changes in the way they manage their businesses (see Case Study 2: Brownells on page 138).

In some cases Lean but Agile requires new processes. Many of these revolve around placing less reliance on full-time employees and more reliance on various combinations of alternative workers. For example, an organization may initiate knowledge-management programs to retain intellectual capital and identity because an increasing chunk of its workers are involved only when needed. They may also work for other organizations.

CASE STUDY 1: ACME CONSULTING

Acme* Consulting provides talent-management software and consulting services. Acme outsources its software development to a primary contractor in the
United States and to secondary contractors in South America and Asia. Using
multiple contractors provides greater scalability, access to more specialists, and
competitive pricing. Software development requires a high degree of coordina-
tion between developers as they all work with the same code base. The primary
contractor coordinates on behalf of Acme when the secondary contractors are
utilized. Each of the contractors in turn has an agile resource structure made
up of full-time employees as well as their own contract workforce, which is utilized as needed. Acme also uses full-time and contract talent-management
consultants who work with Acme's clients. The consultants are empowered to
find and utilize other resources to assist them with their deliverables as long
as quality standards are maintained or exceeded and Acme's costs are not
impacted.

Internal knowledge-management systems are critical for maintaining company continuity. All assignments done by contractors, large or small, are documented in a numbered, dated database created for each Acme client. Initially,
the requirements for each assignment are carefully specified in detail. These requirement documents are not encumbered with pages of legal requirements and
disclaimers. Instead they are designed to include everything the contractor
might need or want to know to assist with completing the work efficiently, including reference documents that may be helpful. Acme and contractors jointly
estimate required levels of labor and cost for each project. Documentation is
regularly maintained as each assignment progresses. Acme staff meets virtually with each active contractor weekly to review and document progress as well
as to discuss new assignments. At the time of completion of the work, the contractor adds technical information that would assist in addressing a similar
issue in the future. The result is a complete history of work done for each client.
The database is searchable (across all Acme clients) by either Acme or present
or future contractors and therefore provides a terrific resource to speed future
similar assignments and to help new contractors get up to speed more quickly.
The assignment database is supplemented by a SharePoint site that is used for
project management as well as to house in-depth technical documents that include product information and procedures.

Acme prioritizes the development of long-term relationships with contractors.
Contractors highly value regular, ongoing work. Acme benefits from the deep knowledge its long-term contractors gain of Acme's products, from higher engagement
and greater personal accountability, and preferential pricing. Further, the nature of
the contractor relationship incents Acme contractors to always be seeking more
work from Acme, in contrast to a traditional employment relationship, where an in-

dividual's income doesn't appreciably increase along with workload. The tenure of Acme's contractors averages more than five years, greater than that of a typical employee workforce.

Of course, on occasion, business needs for Acme or its contractors are best met by making a change. Either party may terminate the work contract at any time and for any reason, without fault or acrimony, but the contract provides for a six-month transition period. During the transition contractors and Acme continue working together closely and cooperatively to smoothly transition work to new contractors. Contractors continue to be paid their normal rates during the transition period. After the transition is complete, relationships are maintained. In the future, Acme and the contractor may once again work together.

---

*"Acme" is a pseudonym.

More often, Lean but Agile requires variations in current processes. Every organization already has approaches for scheduling work. Practices are already in place for selecting and developing employees and managing careers. Lean but Agile organizations encourage a close examination and questioning of all processes. They support creative new approaches that may fly in the face of the way business has been conducted in the past. For example, Brownells (Case Study 2) has discontinued performance reviews for salaried employees, who no longer get a rating or ranking. Brownells is carefully building toward eliminating ratings for hourly workers too. Unlike an organization that uses some of these static processes, a Lean but Agile organization can be expected to look different every year as it evolves because Lean but Agile companies respond quickly to constantly changing environmental, competitive, and economic factors.

There are many Lean but Agile principles and practices that organizations can apply to help them become more effective and efficient, especially in an environment of constantly changing conditions. The principles are best when applied regularly to work prioritization, work assignments, and the practice of human resources and talent management. In this chapter we discuss the Lean but Agile principles and practices that can be integrated into daily management. First, we will review general principles and practices of a Lean but Agile organization. Then we examine Lean but Agile alterations to people-management practices, including staffing, retention, learning and development, performance management, and succession planning.

Quick Review of Three Foundational Principles of Lean but Agile

Three Lean but Agile building blocks that we have emphasized throughout the book bear a quick review. They are (1) focus on strategic, high-impact work; (2) build a talent pool; and (3) use alternative workers.

Focus on Strategic, High-Impact Work

A surprisingly large percentage of work (more than half) done in most organizations is not essential to the mission. Some work is tied to the mission but does not really have much impact. Little is achieved by implementing the practices described in this chapter if the optimized work is not important work.

Understanding the work means ensuring that it flows from organizational strategy or objectives, translating it into performance goals and metrics, and communicating all of this clearly to workers. It also means specifying and documenting work processes and the time and resources required to complete the work. Specifying and documenting the work helps in getting employees and alternative workers up to speed quickly.

Build a Talent Pool

We have defined a *workforce* as all the persons currently completing assignments for an organization, and the *talent pool* as all the individuals (or organizations with individuals) that are prequalified for work assignments for today or the future. The talent pool includes everyone currently working for the organization and a potentially much larger group of other individuals who could make important contributions eventually. A talent pool identifies individuals with needed capabilities *before* they are needed, along with associated costs and availability to the organization. Talent pool members may be full-time or part-time, employees or alternative workers. Their performance history, development, and availability are consistently monitored.

Consider how little most organizations know about their workforces, information that is critical for deploying them wisely. Typically, even less is known about workers who are in the talent pool but not in the current workforce. If you do not know the talents as well as the associated costs of your current workforce and talent pool, you cannot identify the resources with the best ROI for an assignment or optimize the use of your workforce.

Whereas today an organization might keep tabs on one hundred full-time workers and a small number of job candidates, in a more agile reincarnation, it could be managing a far larger talent pool. Some will be part-time. Others will be called only when needed. And some may never be given assignments. A significant percentage of the talent pool may be located remotely, possibly with many dispersed around the globe.

Like a succession-planning pool, a talent pool benefits from containing a larger number of members than is likely to be needed. Having a large and diverse talent pool provides the advantage of greater choice for today's and tomorrow's talent needs, but possibly more important, it provides the *flexibility* needed to more effectively deal with the considerable uncertainties that will impact future talent needs.

Use Alternative Workers to Help Manage Variable Demand and Unpredictability

By *alternative workers* we mean those who are not full-time employees. Instead, they may be part-time employees, contract workers, consultants, freelancers, retirees, or domestic or international outsourcers. There are many other possibilities detailed in chapter 4. The use of alternative workforce arrangements is steadily increasing. Some of today's alternative practices, however, are really not new but were actually commonplace in the past. In the early part of the 1900s, as many as half of manufacturing employees were contractors. Similarly, sales were often outsourced, similar to how auto manufacturers outsource sales to car dealerships in the United States. That full-time employees are an expensive, inflexible, fixed cost is widely understood. Payroll must be met. The portion of employee total rewards at risk (for example, bonuses, raises, commissions) is typically small, particularly on the downside, and employee termination costs are often high. And yet varying work demand is almost inevitable for all business, if for no other reason than the peaks and valleys of the economy. Even when work demand overall from year to year is stable, many organizations have significant cyclical demand. Accounting firms have busy seasons. Mortgage banks tend to have a high call volume from customers on the first day, the fifteenth day, and the last day of the month. Hospital emergency rooms tend to have a higher number of severely intoxicated patients on weekend evenings, which, when combined with other medical conditions, often requires more staff time and more attention to work schedules. Staffing up with a full-time workforce to meet peak demand means that there will be excessive labor costs during the valleys of demand. Similarly, specialists often are needed only part-time. Additional costs of overstaffing may accrue, such as institutionalization of wasteful work rules or turnover of employees with high motivation to achieve.

Increasingly, organizations use full-time employees to meet continuing demands and alternative workers to meet variable demands. There are additional opportunities to use alternative workers even in roles that traditionally have been reserved for full-time staff, and many of these opportunities are discussed in the remainder of this chapter.

Pros and Cons of Contract Workers Versus Employees

Contract workers (CWs) are a growing percentage of alternative workers, and the use of CWs such as consultants, freelancers, and temporary labor alongside employees (EMs) represents one of the most significant opportunities for an organization aspiring to become Lean but Agile.

A CW works under the terms of a contract with different legal and tax obligations than those associated with employees. Organizations have considerable leeway in defining the CW relationship. The work itself or length of labor can be precisely defined, and the contract often contains a flexible termination clause that may be invoked without expensive, negative consequences to a company. CWs may agree to complete a particular job. There may be sanctions if they do not. Work contracts typically define beneficial requirements to the organization such as confidentiality, return of company intellectual and physical property, and noncompete clauses.

What primary forces drive the reduction of EMs and the increase of CWs? Briefly:

■   EMs are often more costly than CWs. It is not just high fixed wages or salaries. Benefits add an additional 30 to 40 percent, on average, and overhead cost can be equal to or greater than salaries. Older employees are often even more expensive given their higher compensation and benefit costs, and their higher cost may be accompanied by decreasing productivity and increasingly obsolete skills.

■   EMs are essentially fixtures in a variable world. It is hard to forecast how much talent will be needed tomorrow.

■   Developing talent internally is expensive, and it is also risky because the talent may not stay with the organization very long, a situation analogous to one individual purchasing a bond and another receiving the dividends. Many of the old incentives for employees to remain with an employer for their career (for example, pensions, security) are no longer in play, while new incentives to leave (for example, increased risk of becoming obsolete) have driven median employee tenure among younger workers to less than three years. Hiring of external resources as needed is often an attractive alternative to risky internal development.

■   Increasingly, in this information age, EMs make up the lion's share of organizational budgets and therefore the best opportunity to cut costs.

■   New computer and communication technologies facilitate alternative work arrangements that would not have been feasible in the past.

Before considering the use of CWs, legal requirements must be reviewed. Depending on the jurisdiction, classifying someone as a CW may limit the supervision, tools, and facilities that can be provided. There are potential liabilities such as back pay and fines associated with treating a person as a CW when the government deems the person to be an EM. Employer withholding of employee pay is good for government coffers, while the irregular pay of CWs makes it more difficult to implement such withholding. In short, favorable government regulations pertaining to CWs are unlikely anytime soon.

External labor market talent surpluses or shortages must be considered. During a surplus, it is easier to find talent on the outside at a reasonable price. In the case of a severe talent shortage, unless organizations are willing to pay top dollar for talent, there may be little choice for them other than to "grow their own." Further, organizations will want to take special care to retain current talent that is in demand.

Here are some helpful guidelines for determining whether EMs or CWs are most advantageous and the proper EM/CW ratio within the organization. Use EMs when:

■   You wish to retain talented individuals in key roles and you have powerful incentives at your disposal that are typically associated today with

employment. EM positions are highly valued because of the security provided by a dependable monthly income. Beyond that, companies may entice
workers with job security, health benefits, tax sharing, profit sharing, pensions,
and valuable credentials and/or work experience. Most of these same benefits
could (in theory) be offered in a CW arrangement, but the mechanisms for
providing these incentives to a CW are less established.

■   You have long-term, consistent work to complete. EMs may cost less
than CWs in this circumstance. For example, a CW software developer at $100
per hour for 2,000 hours a year (essentially full-time) would cost $200,000 per
year, whereas her salary as an EM would probably be only half that. Benefits
increase the cost of an employee, but the EM can still have an overall price
advantage.

■   You cannot offer total rewards that are competitive within the market, but you can offer a significant pay increase to an internal employee and
still pay below the market rate.

■   The role involves particularly proprietary or confidential work.

■   You want to reduce the chance that a valued performer will be working for other organizations—particularly competitors.

■   You have current EMs with the skill set, and it makes sense to redeploy
them because the value of other work is greater than their current work.

■   You have an organizational mandate to fill a certain percentage of
jobs from within.

The use of CWs allows an organization to ramp up or down more quickly
or move in new directions. To borrow the common nautical metaphor, a
speedboat can turn much more quickly than a battleship. Use CWs when:

■   You have variable work demand. You cannot predict with certainty
how much work you will have. As we have said, it is generally best not to staff
with EMs beyond minimum needs.

■   You wish to minimize fixed costs.

■   You want a specialist, and the assignment is short-term and/or a
specialist is very expensive.

■   Internal staff would need development to do certain assignments.

■ Your work processes have been engineered to be reasonably simple and taught quickly. Alternatively, processes are well-specified and the behaviors of effective performers have been identified so that it is easier and quicker to onboard people and move them quickly to a high level of performance. Or, technology has been employed to control or reduce work and create a more or less foolproof process.

■ Local legal requirements make it difficult to lay off a worker, or perhaps workers receive tenure or quasi-guaranteed employment after several years.

■ You want to try out a worker for a period to see how she performs.

■ The best candidates prefer contract work.

We have looked at some of the most important considerations in deciding whether an EM or a CW is preferable for a given role, but these are not hard-and-fast rules. Many common assumptions about situations that are most appropriate for an EM or a CW are ripe for consideration. What *really* will retain a valued worker better, a long-term contract or a full-time employment position? Does it make more sense to invest in the development of employees or contractors? Do you really know that an EM will be more engaged than a CW? More knowledgeable? More productive?

Lean but Agile organizations creatively optimize all their work relationships. For example, an organization with EMs may gain agility through cross-training, furloughs, or savvy scheduling of certain tasks during slow periods. Alternatively, organizations may structure CW positions to include job security, career development, profit sharing, and many other benefits associated traditionally with EMs. Organizational and individual worker preferences play a role in making decisions about which work relationships are most advantageous.

Preserve the Core Identity of the Organization

Every effective organization has a mission, a strategy, processes, and relationships that define it. These create a core identity of the organization. They are maintained, modified when advantageous, and eventually passed on to new leaders and individual contributors to maintain. In an environment where CWs and outsourcers take on an increasing amount of an organization's work, it is natural to question how core identity, core competency, and continuity can be properly maintained. Similarly, as organizations downsize, it is wise to question how much is being lost that cannot easily be regained; that is, how much meat is being cut along with the fat? The current prevailing wisdom is that positions that are "core to the business" should be populated with full-time EMs.

Core roles have been defined as those responsible for maintaining the core capabilities and value proposition of the organization. That is, if a company's competitive advantage lies in its ability to innovate, to manage its supply chain, or to offer superior customer service, then persons in positions most responsible for the value proposition are considered core. For example, one insurance company considers leadership and three roles (actuarial, pharmacy, and nursing) to be core to its business. The same company has prioritized development for leaders and four types of "transformational" workers, that is, those with customer contact, data for decisions, provider engagement, and product innovation.[1] Special emphasis is placed on worker selection, onboarding, development, rewards, and retention for the targeted workers.

Retaining people in core roles is one way to maintain organizational continuity, and it has arguably been the primary way for most organizations. It might be assumed that a full-time position locks up the knowledge, skills, time, contributions, and loyalty of highly valued contributors. Further, organizations are loathe to share their competitive advantage (CWs might work for anyone) with other companies, particularly competitors.

And yet it is reasonable to question the assumption that it is better to staff core positions with EMs than with CWs. Employee *retention* is the foremost concern. If EMs' tenures are short, then former employees take core knowledge and skills along with the company's development investment in them to the competition (or start their own competitive venture) just as readily as a CW.

Employee tenure and retention data are not encouraging. The percentage of workers with long-tenure jobs (ten years or more) has dropped sharply over the past twenty years,[2] and the rate of dismissals has doubled for older workers with significant tenure. Younger baby boomers (those born between years 1957 and 1964) change jobs on average every two years during their first fifteen to twenty years of employment. More generally, of those who started a job in the 1990s, 40 percent saw the job end in less than a year, and only 30 percent saw it last more than five years. The U.S. Bureau of Labor Statistics[3] reports that the median tenure for EMs in the private sector from 2000 to 2010 ranged from 3.2 to 4.0 years, but these results were skewed higher by older workers born before 1957. The data show that more skilled workers (typically the ones that are more likely to be in positions considered to be core) were no more likely to stay than less skilled workers. In fact, high school graduates with no college had slightly higher tenure than college graduates, possibly in part because the college graduates had more marketable skills and were able to find other jobs more easily. Unlike CWs, few EMs who voluntarily leave organizations have signed noncompete agreements.

Quitting voluntarily no longer has the same consequences (or negative connotations with possible future employers) it once had. Formerly when many employees were covered by pensions, becoming fully invested could take five years, and maximizing the pension could take thirty or more years. Whereas 84 percent of workers were covered by pension plans in 1980, that number had decreased to 33 percent by 2006.[4] Similarly, whereas previously the best way for salary growth was to get regular raises through job tenure with the same employer, by the early 1990s those who moved to different employers did as well—and in some cases better.

The importance of maintaining mission, strategy, processes, and relationships cannot be disputed. But counting on EMs as the primary mechanism for doing that in today's environment may be risky. Further, given the potential advantages of CWs, it makes little sense to categorically reject CWs for those positions. Putting in place effective retention strategies applicable to all types of workers may be a wiser strategy.

Next we look at a complementary approach, knowledge management, to maintain organization knowledge.

Knowledge Management

Institutional knowledge is maintained both in written documents and in people. Organizations preserve information on current work processes and practices, and contacts and relationships with customers, partners, and affiliates. They maintain historical records such as specific details of customer engagements, lessons learned, and best practices. Much of this information may be tacit knowledge that is held in the heads of individuals but not formally captured in standard operating procedures or other documentation.

Institutional knowledge tends to be associated more with some positions than others. Brownells (Case Study 2) segments jobs into three categories:

knowledge, support, and contingent. Brownells' knowledge jobs are those that take significant time (perhaps years) for an individual to become proficient. Some knowledge may be gained through formal education. But typically much of it must also be gained on the job within Brownells. By contrast, some jobs can be learned quickly and workers can be reasonably proficient as rapidly as one day. Brownells prefers that knowledge workers be EMs, but it makes liberal use of CWs in support and contingent positions.

Organizations can decrease worker time to full proficiency by capturing tacit information and making it explicit. Undocumented work processes are a good place to start. Processes can be documented, and previously tacit information can be made available through training and databases. "Tricks of the trade," "rules of thumb," or best practices also should be captured. Supervisors and job incumbents can be asked to answer questions such as what it means to "go the extra mile" or to reflect on the approaches used by top performers to identify tacit best practices. These best practices can be documented as performance standards in performance-management systems.

Knowledge-management approaches enable more flexibility in work assignments and more redundancy. Workers can be brought up to speed on new assignments more quickly and economically, and it lessens the impact when workers with longtime knowledge leave the organization. As knowledge management improves, it becomes easier to employ CWs effectively.

CASE STUDY 2: BROWNELLS, INC., AGILE WORKFORCE INITIATIVE

Brownells is a third-generation, family-owned company in the heartland of the United States with about 250 employees. Brownells has been providing quality gunsmithing tools, parts, and accessories to gunsmiths, hunters, the military, law enforcement, and government agencies for more than seventy years. The company is guided by the value proposition established by CEO Frank Brownell: Selection, Service and Satisfaction.

Current president Pete Brownell is overseeing rapid growth. Recently he asked function heads to identify support needed for them to successfully meet their goals and cope with the increasing pace and volume of business. Almost unanimously, managers asked for support to increase *speed and agility*. Brownells uses *hunting* as an analogy that can prime them for speed and agility. The steps are:

1. *Pick your hunt: Strategic discipline = customer focus.* In other words, Brownells' strategy is to provide successful customer experiences. Brownells empowers and holds staff accountable for making this happen.

2. *Choose the right gear: Reconfigurable organization.* Conditions can change rapidly and the company needs an agile workforce that can quickly adjust.

3. *Practice and prepare: Tailored talent management.* Brownells has coordinated its talent-management practices to support both their singular focus on customer experience and an agile workforce. See below for further description of staffing, training, knowledge management, and compensation practices.

4. *Know the habitat or get a good guide: Navigate with knowledgeable partners.* Brownells has built a flexible, scalable network of partners. They feel that being structured as a network makes them more resilient and innovative than if they were monolithic.

5. *End of the day, a successful hunt and no unintended targets: Don't forget the mission.* The impact of this rule can be seen in many of the company job descriptions and company rules. They are kept general because Brownells doesn't want to draw a small box around what is expected. A satisfactory customer experience is everyone's job, and the company doesn't want employees obsessing over small details at the expense of the mission.

Reorganization

Growing by acquisition as well as organically, Brownells has settled on various people strategies to effectively manage its growth. First, Brownells reorganized and created a centralized support services group to drive operational efficiencies and leverage its strengths in process design and management. HR, IT, finance, business development, supply chain, call center, and order fulfillment all fall under the umbrella of shared services. Second, it is developing an *agile* talent strategy to accommodate the current steep growth trajectory, but also to be better prepared to cope with a variety of future scenarios. For example, the organization wishes to be agile enough to cope well with increases in demand for some product lines accompanied by stability or decreases in others. Brownells is in an industry that is strongly impacted by political and regulatory changes, so contingency plans are particularly important.

Job Types

Human resources decided that in order for the company to create an agile workforce, it would need to focus its limited resources on workers who are best positioned to drive innovation. HR reviewed jobs at Brownells and categorized them into three buckets: knowledge, support, and contingent. Brownells' agile workforce initiative is implemented differently based on these job types.

Knowledge jobs require a significant knowledge base attained typically through a combination of college, other advanced training, and job experience. Knowledge jobs tend to have limited operating procedures and therefore are more amenable to improvement by job incumbents. Most exempt (salaried) jobs, including those in marketing, finance, IT, and management, are examples.

Support jobs are typically more clerical in nature, such as most positions in accounts payable and accounts receivable and most call center jobs, as well as team leads in order fulfillment. They do require a knowledge base, but much of that knowledge is gained by workers on the job at Brownells.

Contingent jobs are very structured and most are partially automated. Many of these jobs are in order fulfillment. A revamped worker onboarding process has paid off; Brownells can now train an order picker in one day or less. Some contingent work at Brownells is full-time and some is part-time; most is onsite but some is at home.

Cross-Training

Cross-training is a key agile workforce initiative at Brownells, particularly for contingent and support workers. Brownells builds agility into its largest departments (call center and order fulfillment) by training workers to operate effectively in any job in the department. For example, in the call center workers are trained to sell different product lines. Naturally there are many laws and guidelines that govern firearm sales. Over time, employees are taught to deal with more complex, regulation-laden areas such as government sales and international sales. In the order fulfillment area, packers learn to pick orders, pickers learn to pack, and either may be trained to assist with other fulfillment areas such as kitting, shipping, or receiving.

Professional workers also may be cross-trained. For example, marketing copywriters formerly wrote for one product line. Language and writing style differ for police agencies and recreational user product lines. Today, copywriters are taught to write and speak in the different styles and vocabularies required by the FBI, local police agencies, and recreational firearms users. Appropriate cross-training is determined on a case-by-case basis. For example, given the scarcity of highly skilled gunsmiths, gunsmiths can provide the most value by working primarily in their own specialty areas.

Brownells is committed to maintaining a core group of people who will continue to play multiple roles regardless of company growth. Besides adding to agility, multiple role players are more likely to see the "big picture." Keeping the big picture in mind helps to keep the company coordinated and additionally can often lead to more innovation.

There has been worker resistance on occasion to having people work in multiple roles. Brownells has made a concerted effort to develop company norms that are supportive of cross-training. Similarly, part-timers initially felt like they were not as appreciated as the full-timers. Frontline supervisors were trained to give feedback to all workers about their significance and to emphasize the importance of the part-timers to the company.

Part-Time Staff

Brownells needs flexibility in its staffing to deal with significant peaks and valleys in work and resulting worker demand. The company typically experiences a rush of orders on Monday and predictable peaks in demand at different times during the day. Further, the firearms industry is seasonal. Orders in the northern hemisphere begin ramping up in November, peak in March, and then slow down somewhat during the summer months. In order to address the uneven demand, Brownells has begun using more part-time workers.

Several years ago there were no part-timers. There was resistance to using part-timers because it wasn't the Brownells way and there was a belief that in its rural area Brownells couldn't find people who wanted part-time work and flexible hours. The company slowly eased into using part-timers and the results were good, so part-time staff continued to grow. Currently about 40 percent of call center and order fulfillment staff are part-time employees. Jeannine Kosman, Brownells' director of knowledge management, estimates that about half of the part-timers would prefer more hours, and they are the first persons considered when Brownells adds full-time positions.

Daily Work Clearly Linked to Strategy

Brownells has made a commitment to have all employees understand the company strategic plan, and what that plan means on a day-to-day basis for each worker. Brownells has found that hosting a splashy event to roll out the company strategy doesn't work nearly as well as meeting with managers to ensure that they understand the strategic plan, their department objectives, and their measurements. Then the strategy is driven down to all employees through communication and reward.

A tour of the Brownells plant and offices reveals pervasive computer monitors mounted high in every department. They show the goals for the day as well as what has been achieved up to the moment. For example, staff members can see the number of orders processed by the call center, order fill rates by line, and supply chain metrics. So, if the goal for the day is 90 percent same-day order fulfillment, employees see that 50 percent of the orders need to be filled by 11 a.m., and they can see if they are ahead, behind, or on schedule.

All the staff shares the fruits of company success. Hourly employees receive quarterly bonuses that are based on team performance. Directors meet with hourly employees to discuss how they did compared to the plan, how the company is performing on financial metrics, and where that puts them on bonus. The rewards go beyond that; company growth also means Brownells can fill more full-time positions, which the company has committed to fill from the ranks of interested part-timers.

Recent employee survey results reflect that the company-wide initiative to help people see the connection between what they do and where the company is going has been successful. The company has exceeded 98 percent of employees who now agree that "My job is important to the company" and "My Job connects to the company strategy."

Additional Ramifications of Knowledge, Support, and Contingent Workers

Succession planning is being set up for critical knowledge workers at all levels of the organization, not just in leadership positions. Brownells understands that certain employees have important historical knowledge that the company doesn't want to lose, so knowledge transfer and succession is being planned for the knowledge positions that exist in all areas of the company.

Brownells endeavors to hire learning-agile (it calls them "smart") workers, particularly for knowledge worker roles. Even for contingent positions, Brownells looks to hire individuals who are both capable and flexible enough to learn and work on different product lines.

Workforce Agility Extends to Worker Mindset

Traditionally Brownells was good at customer service and operational efficiency at a transaction level. Now it is moving toward a higher level of customer understanding. Staff members are asked to think holistically about what Brownells customers need overall, rather than just taking an order. For example, originally the company offered gunsmith tools and fulfilled just the requested order. Leadership started considering the question, "Who else do our customers call after they get off the phone with us?" This led to the development of new products and services, which are now offered proactively when gunsmith tools are ordered.

Today, Brownells workers are being asked to develop an agile *mindset*, not only about what the customer needs but to think more flexibly about what their jobs entail. In other words, their job is not captured by a static job description filled with responsibility statements. Instead, their tasks are better defined as whatever it takes to achieve their goals. This is reinforced by making sure employees are given opportunities to work in their natural areas of strength, which turns on the "engagement" switch. Brownells is creating an environment where all workers are encouraged and rewarded for thinking like owners. That mentality may be just what is needed to get to the next level of workforce agility.

Source Talent Internally or Externally

Over the years the pendulum has swung back and forth between whether talent was sourced within the organization or from outside. As discussed in chapter 1, circumstances in the post–World War II period from 1946 to 1970 favored internal development and sourcing of talent. Since then it has become easier to fill positions with external hires.

Upon first glance, one might assume that Lean but Agile organizations would favor looking outside for talent. Lean organizations tend to have fewer levels of hierarchy, in part because they do less low-impact work and also be-cause with fewer people there is less need for a middle management layer to maintain communications and organizational oversight. In a less hierarchi-cal organization the steps from one level to the next may be larger and more difficult to negotiate, making it more difficult for a promoted internal worker to succeed. Further, each job filled internally creates a new gap, the so-called chain of moves (sometimes called the domino effect) issue. Assuming that Lean but Agile organizations have reduced how much work is unrelated to the strategy, moving someone in a Lean but Agile organization can create a large gap to be filled, worsening the chain-of-moves problem.

Although Lean but Agile organizations tend toward greater utilization of alternative work arrangements and a higher percentage of CWs than in the past, this does *not* imply a preference for external hiring. In fact, a talent pool (see chapter 3) is largely effective because it offers the advantages of internal hiring without many of the disadvantages. The Lean but Agile organization redefines "hiring internally" to mean selecting talent from the talent pool. These are the benefits:

■ More accurate assessments of candidate skill sets and fit, which in turn means better performance at work.

■ Reduction of high-cost talent searches and assessments. Developing a talent pool still requires sourcing talent, but it can be done with less expen-sive means when there is less urgency. For example, executive search services are unlikely to be needed.

■ Talent needs are filled very quickly. Each day a role is unfilled could result in lost billings or even a lost client.

■ Worker retention improves. Workers appreciate the benefit of being part of a group (a talent pool) that is given the first opportunity to fulfill as-signments. Improved retention preserves organizational knowledge and ef-fectiveness and worker development investments.

■ Compensation costs may be lower. A 10 to 15 percent raise for an in-ternal hire may be satisfactory to all parties, particularly if further develop-ment is needed, but that can still be less costly than hiring externally.

■ Quicker acculturation of workers. In some cultures outsiders can struggle to find their way.

Lean but Agile Talent Management

Now we turn to a discussion of the Lean but Agile strategies that can be applied regularly to talent management. In times of constrained resources, it is especially important that *all* talent-management practices be effective and that the results be good. A poor hiring decision may be a bit more tolerable when resources are abundant. But when they are lean, the negative impact is felt more acutely.

In the remainder of this chapter, we consider agile work, agile job descriptions, staffing, worker assignment, retention, learning and development, performance planning and review, succession planning, and lean calculations. Some practices we mention are relatively new for most organizations, while some have been commonly used for many years but deserve attention by a Lean but Agile organization. Many practices we discuss take on a different hue in the Lean but Agile organization because they cover a much broader population of workers. That is, they need to be applied to talent pool members, not just the EMs working today for the organization.

Keep in mind that not all practices will apply to all organizations. Further, depending on your locale and type of organization, some may even be prohibited by law or local custom. Therefore, the following practices must be screened for relevance and potential positive impact for your organization and for compliance with legal and contractual requirements. Finally, although the list of practices we cover next is extensive, readers can undoubtedly identify additional practices that will help their organizations become more Lean but Agile.

Agilc Work

Lean but Agile organizations understand which capabilities provide them with their strategic advantage—for example, speed, leadership, innovation, or price. They then follow practices we have discussed in this book to identify lean work, create a lean workforce, and plan for and build their agility. As you know by now, *lean work* is work that plays to strengths and focuses on high-impact activity. A *lean workforce* is one that is designed to complete lean work effectively and efficiently. *Agility* is achieved in large part through frequent work prioritization, the development of a mature talent pool, and an advantageous mix of EMs and CWs.

Most organizations create *annual* plans and goals. The goals may be cascaded down into department and/or individual work plans. Is the typical annual planning and goal-setting process sufficiently detailed and responsive for day-to-day work planning? Given how little the annual plan informs the work of most workers, the answer to the question may well be no.

Much can potentially be learned from agile software development. Traditionally, software has been developed in a "waterfall style," a highly structured and sequential process that begins with a detailed plan designed to optimally achieve desired software capabilities. The process then flows to design, software development, unit and regression testing, and finally verification within the organization. It is a logical process that in many respects is analogous to an organization's annual planning process. However, the waterfall process does not easily accommodate changes in requirements. A change in direction minimally results in wasted time and money and may require that the project be started over again. Similarly, the approach is not very adaptable if funding or resources are reduced or if the project is terminated for any other reason. In short, it may be difficult to salvage much value from the project unless it is brought to completion. Further, the process is not flexible enough to incorporate the inevitable insights—the learning curve—that occur along the way as work is completed. Finally, studies have shown that typically more than 50 percent of functions within the software are either never used or rarely used, which means that there is also a lot of wasted work and expense.[5]

Agile software development is an alternative to the waterfall method. Agile development is accomplished in a series of short cycles that typically range from one to four weeks each, compared to a waterfall project that lasts months or even years. Far less time is spent on the initial documentation of every detail in the specifications because a smaller amount of work is being done. The specifications are supplemented by regular conversations between the developers and their clients. Each cycle focuses on the highest priority at the time so the process can accommodate incorrect forecasts or rapidly changing priorities. Usable work is produced each cycle, with the result that a change of direction does not leave the organization with a partially developed product with no value. In sum, agile development combines a disciplined process of evaluating and prioritizing work regularly together with the flexibility to change direction at the end of each cycle. Its principles might be applied to many types of work. Indeed, it is instructive for Lean but Agile work and workforce planning.

The agile approach helps build strong, innovative work teams. Insights of all team members are welcomed and considered. Frequent communications are built into the process, and goals are explained at the start of each cycle. Since the goals are limited, they are more easily understood. Individual and team reinforcement occurs regularly. The length of the planning cycle that works best is selected. Shorter cycles are more appropriate where priorities change rapidly.

We do not mean to present agile software development as a panacea. It can be difficult to transition to the approach. For example, when services are purchased (whether from a contractor or an employee), buyers typically are seeking a *specific* product or deliverable in a *fixed* time and at a *fixed* price. To take a simple example, if we contract with a construction company to build a house, we expect that the builder will deliver the house with the agreed features at the agreed time and cost. However, an agile work process may offer none of these guarantees. The deliverable is likely to evolve, and the time frames and costs may only be set for each stage of the work, which might be organized in two-week cycles. Some internal stakeholders may be open to an agile work process. But it may be difficult to convince external customers of the merits of the process when compared with fixed deliverables, time frames, and costs.

The applicability of the approach may come down to the nature of the work being done and the customer. It may be a very good approach in situations where work requests are unpredictable, requests change rapidly, communication is good, and trust is high. However, where work is repetitive, predictable, and well-understood, or when you are working directly with customers, more traditional approaches may be required.

Agile Job Descriptions

The traditional job description is a potential inhibitor of Lean but Agile work. It is more focused on activities than strategy or results. It is also a relatively static document that does not adjust well to changing priorities. Some important work may not fall within any job description, and there is always the potential for the "it's not my job" syndrome, even if the job description includes the ubiquitous caveat "other duties as assigned." Further, the job description often lists work that no longer is very important, but the job incumbent may feel compelled (or may prefer) to do it, and more important tasks do not receive their due.

Lean but Agile organizations seek to maximize the impact of each worker. Many healthcare facilities are a good example. Profit margins are tight, staffing is lean, and highly trained professionals are expensive resources. Hospitals have learned to transition certain tasks, such as weighing of patients or taking blood pressure, away from skilled nurses and over to lower-cost nursing assistants. In this manner more nursing time is spent on high-value activities. Additionally, nurses specialize to increase their expertise and improve patient services. A labor and delivery nurse does different work than one in med/surgery. Although most nurses can start IVs, some will naturally be more proficient than others and can be called upon to assist under particularly challenging circumstances. When work is broken down into key roles instead of lumped together in job descriptions, it is easier to optimize job assignments based on employee strengths, availability, and cost.

In addition to assigning individuals more flexibly without the constraints of job descriptions, *shorter assignments* are another way to optimize. Many companies (legal, accounting, IT, engineering, construction, to mention but a few) already are project-based, and they move resources to new projects according to the greatest need. Worker commitment and retention is likely to increase because employees can see their own impact more clearly and feel more personal ownership of their work. We expect to see an increasing number of organizations divide their work into projects, with people redeployed into new roles frequently.

Staffing

Now we turn to Lean but Agile strategies and tactics that can be applied to *worker selection*. Traditional *employee* selection focuses on filling positions, whereas with Lean but Agile the purpose of *worker selection* is to find workers for the organization's *talent pool*. We have recommended that candidates for the talent pool be assessed using *five talent indicators*: (1) performance history, (2) competence, (3) education, (4) experience, and (5) personal preferences/fit (see chapter 3 for a complete discussion of the five talent indicators). The advantages of going with qualified talent pool members (whether EMs or CWs) versus outsiders are:

- *Performance, quality, and worker fit can be evaluated much more accurately.* Even if you have not worked with a talent pool member before, you are likely to have more complete data as you track him or her over time than will be immediately available for an outsider. Better evaluations mean that the organization will have a more competent, successful workforce.

■   *Talent pool candidates can be identified, their interest confirmed, and selection finalized much faster.* Today there are companies that can fill a professional position within hours of an opening and have them at work the next day. In a tight labor market, the speed advantage provided by a talent pool is even greater.

■   *Selecting from the talent pool reduces or eliminates the high costs associated with external searches, including recruitment, processing, and search fees.*

■   *Talent pool members are likely to require significantly less time to get up to speed with their work.*

Selecting a worker for the talent pool does not dictate that he or she will be doing any work for the organization either immediately or, for that matter, ever. We are merely qualifying individuals to work for our organization; whether they are assigned work is another matter (see the "Worker Assignment" section on page 153). Unlike traditional employee selection, the goal is to identify workers *before* they are needed.

Building a talent pool in advance may raise a concern of wasted effort, particularly for those workers who are never used. Further, it seems to violate the principle that resources not be expended until a need is certain. However, there is *great value* in avoiding the mini-crisis that occurs in most organizations every time there is an opening for a worker. There are of course caveats; we are not suggesting that qualified workers be identified *years in advance* (see just-in-time worker selection tactics in the following list) of a forecasted need, or that the talent pool be populated for every position. Finally, talent pool members are recruited because they are able to fulfill one or more very valuable roles; they are typically not recruited in correspondence to one job description.

Here now are Lean but Agile staffing tactics:

1. *First populate the talent pool with persons that fulfill critical roles.* Identify roles or jobs that have a high impact on essential work and manage those first in your talent pool. This is called talent segmentation. If necessary, talent for less essential or lower-impact work can be found outside your talent pool.

2. *Forecast talent requirements, but keep the forecast period reasonably short.* Lean but Agile organizations seek to be agile to meet talent needs, present and future. Future talent needs require forecasting of future workload, which is done based on current trends as well as future strategy and plans. Based on the demographics of your workforce such as age and typical turnover and retirement behavior, talent replacement needs can be forecasted. A two-year forecast of talent demand is more likely to be accurate than a ten-year forecast. Sometimes staffing activity can be adjusted to artificially create a shorter forecast. For example, if currently you hire all college graduates for the year during the most common graduation period (April through June in the United States), consider breaking hiring into thirds, with one-third each at the end of spring, summer, and fall/winter graduations. This has the effect of shortening the forecast period.

Certain circumstances require more lead time and a longer forecast. For example, the U.S. Veterans Administration is the largest employer of nurses in the United States, and it has a variety of programs in place to ensure itself an adequate supply. One very-long-range program encourages high school students to consider nursing as a career.[6] The VA creates a long-term talent forecast but updates it annually. There would be nothing to prevent even more frequent updates of the forecast, potentially whenever underlying assumptions change. Workforce planning tools can assist in making frequent forecast tweaking a reasonably simple matter.

3. *Develop ideal candidate models prior to searching for talent.* We noted earlier (in chapter 3) that a worker at the 80th percentile can be expected on average to be about twice as productive as one at the 20th percentile. When an organization is lean, selecting a worker that is a poor fit can be particularly impactful. Although many consider themselves excellent judges of talent, worker selection done without job analysis and proper worker assessment is essentially selection by hunch. It is not much better than random selection. At a minimum, develop a competency model that describes the characteristics of an ideal performer. Even better, create a complete job profile with desired performance history, education, experience, and personal preferences/fit.

4. *Set goals for hiring from your talent pool.* Similar to goals set by some companies for internal hiring, we recommend that you set goals for hiring from your talent pool. Talent pool hiring goals can be more easily met because the talent pool provides opportunities to meet talent needs using

alternative workers or current employees. It is not out of the realm of possibility to eventually fill 90 percent or more of essential worker needs from a mature talent pool.

5. *Set metrics for the quality of your talent pool.* What is the quality of your talent pool? Bench strength, which is used to measure the quality of succession candidates, can also be used to measure the strength of your talent pool. Ideally, candidate strength can be measured on the five talent indicators we have recommended: (1) performance history, (2) competence, (3) education, (4) experience, and (5) personal preferences/fit. If you plan to start with just one or two of these measures, then performance history and competence may be good choices. Average performance review scores are easily tracked. For competence, you will want to measure average proficiency of talent pool members for positions where they are most likely to be used. Assuming competency models are in place that include required competencies, competency weights, and required levels of performance (for example, from beginner to expert), talent-management applications can calculate average proficiency scores for different functions. A lower average proficiency indicates an area where there is a need to improve the talent pool. Over time, it is wise to set goals for continual strengthening of talent pool scores.

6. *Adjust your talent strategy based on talent shortages or labor surpluses.* Optimum talent strategy is impacted by labor surpluses and shortages. For example, during periods of surplus, you may be able to reduce internal development and be less compulsive about having backups in the talent pool. However, even in periods of labor surplus, there are likely to be some difficult-to-find skill sets where talent planning is required. It is important to regularly evaluate the skill sets your company needs and build bench strength well in advance for those that are scarce. You may need to search longer or develop these skills internally.

7. *Staff only for levels that you are certain will be required.* Overstaffing of employees is generally more costly and risky than understaffing. Overstaffing results in higher than necessary compensation, benefits, overhead, and employee development costs. Employees may be underutilized as there may be a waiting period before they can be moved into their roles. In addition, there can be retention problems because people will leave if they fear there is too much competition or if they are not given opportunities soon enough. If downsizing is required, there may be severance package

costs, possibly outplacement, the potential for bumping costs as some employees move downward, and a higher risk of litigation.

To help avoid overstaffing, assign a confidence estimate to your talent need projections. For example, if you forecast that you will need one hundred computer programmers but are not absolutely certain, you might want to hire or develop ninety. And if you are not confident at all, you may want to staff or develop only fifty or sixty.

8. *Apply just-in-time (JIT) hiring.* It is too expensive to have people sitting on the bench waiting for work to begin, if even just for a few extra weeks. Your talent pool is the key enabler of JIT hiring, and it provides redundancy at minimal cost.

9. *Consider the value of worker readiness.* A new worker's speed to proficiency, or readiness, impacts organizational agility. Obviously, the faster resources become fully proficient, the sooner the person will become fully productive and the more effectively an organization can respond to change. It is customary to estimate readiness of backups in succession replacement charts to assist with talent planning, and the same concept is valuable for talent pool members. See Figure 6-2 on page 178 for an example of how worker readiness can impact a staffing decision.

10. *Select agile workers.* Persons who are capable of performing more than one critical function are potentially more valuable, particularly if they are employees. Earlier we suggested that you first populate your talent pool with persons who can fill critical roles. Suppose that you identified ten of these. With the help of talent-management software or a simple spreadsheet, you can determine how many of these roles a candidate can fill capably. Those who can fulfill multiple roles give you a more agile workforce, and they can be placed in high-value assignments more often.

11. *Remember, nothing predicts as well as actual performance.* Even the best worker-screening devices are only fallible predictions of potential performance. Even when work history shows that a candidate is promising, the most reliable way to confirm fit is to provide an on-the-job, risk-controlled opportunity to do some work in your environment. The notion of probationary periods for employees is not new, but short probationary periods and weak evaluations may impede decisions. Bringing promising workers on as CWs for sufficient time with clear deliverables can enhance employee staffing decisions.

12. *Let workers suggest where they can contribute.* Rather than hiring for a static job position, have workers provide input on the organizational roles that fit them best, regardless of which roles are currently staffed. This provides a view of the intersection of an individual's capabilities and personal preferences with company needs, their "sweet spot" of fit with your organization. This perspective requires that workers be actively involved in role staffing and assignment. If possible, provide tools (use the same ones that help employees with career development) to help potential new hires make better decisions on good matches for them for deployment within your organization. Of course, you will want to verify their role selections with the other data you have available.

13. *Post your opportunities and needs.* Again, this is not a new idea, but role posting fits well with Lean but Agile. Competition tends to drive better results and lower costs. Workers appreciate additional opportunities. Finally, self-nomination provides valuable information about candidates and may be a good indicator of motivation for the job and interest in career development.

14. *Hire from within your talent pool.* These are the persons whom you have vetted, and you will want to continue to provide incentives for their participation in the pool.

15. *Calculate your most efficient sources of workers.* Traditionally, some organizations source their work candidates from a limited range of universities. For example, in the United States, top-tier law firms may prefer Ivy League (e.g., Harvard or Yale) graduates. Analyses of the fruitfulness of different candidate sources can be very useful. Correlating performance with worker profiles may provide good hints on where to recruit. Two-year degrees? Five years of experience? Civil engineers but not chemical engineers? Are Ivy Leaguers *really* more successful in top law firms than those hired from other universities? Let's give the benefit of the doubt and assume that the firms have confirmed that through appropriate analyses.

16. *Be opportunistic.* Every organization has talent opportunities that allow it to get stronger, reduce worker costs, or become more agile, but it must be attentive and seize the opportunities when they present themselves! Professional sports organizations have scouting functions that are geared toward finding these opportunities, but often all that is really needed is the application of a bit of logic. For example, suppose that another local organization hires primarily new graduates for its technician positions because that

organization is a low payer in the marketplace. Many of the technicians may work at the other company for one to two years and then look for higher wages and/or a more leading-edge organization. This would be a good place to recruit. It could even be an impetus for changing specs for technicians going forward and requiring one to two years of experience. Why absorb the lower productivity and development costs of newly minted technicians when another organization will do it for you?

17. *Take a long-term perspective.* Traditionally, this rule has led to selecting a young worker based on the notion that the younger worker might be in your workforce longer. Tenure data today show that this assumption might not be a good one, but the point is that it is important to take a big-picture, long-term perspective of what an individual is likely to provide your organization.

Even if applicants do not fit well with your needs today, they may deserve spots in your talent pool. Most candidates you review have initial qualifications or they would never have been considered. Before throwing away your time investment, consider if the candidate might eventually be able to play an important role. If so, maintain a relationship the same way you might with worker alumni, who also may come back at a later time to contribute.

Worker Assignment

Lean worker assignment is the process of selecting the optimal human resources from your talent pool to complete the organization's prioritized work. *Optimal assignment* means identifying the right workers to perform each required role at the right cost at any given time. More specifically:

■　Select workers who are well-qualified and highly competent to do the work but are not overqualified.

■　Maximize the value of the work each individual performs at any given time. The best solution is a function of an individual's capabilities, the talents of the other individuals in the talent pool, and the work that needs to be performed at the time.

■　Minimize the costs of the workforce. This should occur in large part through following the first two points, but it also requires consideration of the costs of using employees or alternative workers.

Next we review suggestions for Lean but Agile worker assignment:

1. *Consider mobile talent groups.* This concept increases the options for assigning workers where they can provide the most value. Workers are recruited or developed for a mobile group with the understanding their role is to fill in whenever and wherever needed.

2. *Make contingent work assignments.* This strategy involves contracting for talent *contingent on the need.* For example, ABC Company bids on a project, but there are three other companies also bidding, so staffing up is risky. However, to win the business, ABC must identify the project team, and if the bid is secured, the client will expect ABC to begin immediately. Therefore, ABC assigns qualified CWs to the project *contingent* on winning the business. The CW contracts to be available within twenty-four hours of notification. If the work is lucrative, the CW has availability, and there is an ample supply of other qualified resources, the CW may be amenable. Otherwise, ABC may have to pay a retainer.

3. *Make on-call arrangements.* "Predictably unpredictable" situations are common for many organizations, and on-call resources provide needed flexibility. For example, doctors and nurses are put "on call" to deal with many uncertainties. A bad accident can result in an emergency room "getting slammed." Babies do not always arrive between 9 a.m. and 5 p.m., Monday through Friday. Retirees may be a possible source of "on-call" workers if communication channels are kept open with them.

4. *Consider talent pool portfolios to reduce unpredictability.* Larger organizations may be able to manage inaccuracies in their talent forecasts and resulting talent surpluses or shortages by sharing talent across locations, product lines, or business units. More than likely, some talent need forecasts will be too high and some too low. A shortage of talent in one area can be wiped out by a surplus in another. Although it is more challenging, smaller organizations may be able to apply the portfolio concept by potentially partnering with other compatible organizations.

Retention

Earlier we reviewed data on employee retention trends and showed that, at least in the private sector, the norm is now that people tend to change jobs every two years. Short worker tenure poses a significant problem for most organizations. The cost of turnover has been estimated at one to one-and-a-half times annual salary or higher. Worker retention is often the primary method for maintaining organizational performance, knowledge, identity, relationships, and ultimately competitive advantage. Further, it takes time to gain an ROI on employee onboarding and development. Retaining effective performers is a priority.

As alternative worker arrangements increase, retention of workers, including CWs, may be just as important as retention of EMs. Case Study 1 describes a company that enjoys an average CW tenure in excess of five years. Offering work arrangements that meet workers' needs will itself assist in retention. Retention of all talent pool members is important—including those who have not yet worked for you.

Worker retention in the Lean but Agile organization is really about *maintaining a long-term, respectful, mutually beneficial relationship.* Workers whom you interview but choose not to hire ideally are retained in the talent pool if they demonstrate applicable competencies and a strong record of performance. Similarly, EMs that leave the organization, either through retirement or even to take work elsewhere, are valued alumni who may work again for your organization as an EM or a CW. Even in the case of "good turnover," that is, those cases where an individual is not currently a good fit, maintaining a positive relationship can lead to a favorably disposed advocate for your organization instead of a critic. CWs with long-term relationships with an organization are better positioned to help an organization than CWs who are "one and done." Long-term relationships also benefit CWs.

We turn now to some Lean but Agile worker-retention tactics:

1. *Create a robust career development program.* EMs and CWs seek to grow, keep current, and increase income. Numerous studies document that development opportunities drive retention and are a leading indicator of worker engagement in all countries.[7]

Internal career development systems need to be as good as, if not better than, what is available on the outside. Today, an employee can post a resume in minutes and have several job offers in less than twenty-four hours, replacing the laborious process of getting an application, mailing resumes, and waiting for replies. Company career development systems need to be as easy and as fast.

Job information is the first pillar of robust career development. Internal and external candidates need easy access to this information to offer their services where appropriate. At a minimum, a career development system should include descriptions of the work, education and experience requirements, competency models, any job standards, and work characteristics (such as travel) that help workers determine fit with personal preferences. Mission, current priorities, culture, and typical opportunities available in different functions can also be provided.

The second pillar of career development is a mature talent pool with the worker information we have previously suggested, that is, (1) performance history, (2) competence, (3) education, (4) experience, and (5) personal preferences/fit. It is a conundrum that organizations know more about external job candidates than about their own workers and that as time goes on they often know less about their workers because information about them becomes increasingly outdated. Members of the talent pool should be encouraged and incented to keep their information current. A mature talent pool enables an organization to search for qualified internal candidates or to validly make comparisons with external candidates.

Finally, technology is needed to calculate good matches between the talent pool and work roles, with views available from the individual perspective (what work roles fit me) and the organizational perspective (what workers are a great fit).

Employees routinely state that they do not know of available internal career opportunities, and they cite this when leaving an organization. The lockstep career ladders that were common fifty years ago are mainly gone, both because organizations are leaner and less hierarchical, and because rapid change is anathema to rigid career ladders. However, flexible individual career paths fit well within the Lean but Agile organization. They are aligned with individual strengths and preferences as well as organizational needs, and unlike career ladders, they can take an individual to totally new functions outside the current job family. Individual career paths are easily updated as individual priorities or organizational needs evolve.

2. *Hire internally.* This point was made when we discussed staffing practices, but it bears briefly repeating here. Nothing conveys internal opportunity better than seeing important positions filled by peers or oneself. When executives are hired from outside, they often bring their own teams. This leads to an exodus of existing talent, and those who remain are likely to feel that their future prospects in the organization have dimmed.

3. *Survey your talent pool to identify key threats to retention.* This is a commonplace but effective tool, and it can be extended to CWs and the entire talent pool. If anonymity is properly protected, survey respondents are surprisingly frank about whether or not they expect to leave the organization soon and what would lead them to do so. Alternatively, pose different scenarios and ask employees if they would leave, for example, for a onetime bonus of $1,000, for ten more vacation days, or some other benefit.

4. *Identify retention risks.* Many succession-planning programs identify backups thought to be at risk of leaving the organization soon. Identification of these workers allows a proactive review of contributing factors and an opportunity to retain a significant percentage. Retention risks may be identified by supervisors, by regularly asking individuals about their satisfaction and career intentions or by considering risk factors such as underutilization, overwork, development not accompanied by promotion, or roles with short average tenure. It is wise to calculate or estimate the cost of turnover for different roles and to focus on areas where the cost is high.

5. *Mobility brings competency; competency brings mobility.* Competency and mobility bring to mind the ancient question, "Which came first, the chicken or the egg," as each can create the other, a two-edged sword. Moving workers to different job assignments is one best way to develop workers quickly, but greater competence results in more opportunities to look elsewhere and a higher chance of being recruited. A Watson-Wyatt study confirms that having recently received training is one of the best predictors of turnover.[8] Those who are developed should also be a focus of retention, starting with role assignments that utilize the new skills and commensurate rewards.

6. *Contracts may help retention.* Defining a body of work, standards of performance, a fixed price, and liabilities for breach of contract is commonplace when consultants are retained. The contractor may be responsible for providing qualified replacements if original staff become unable to do the work.

Learning and Development

Employee development has undergone as much if not more of a transition in recent years than any area of talent management. Even the name has morphed from *T&D* (training and development) to *L&D* (learning and development).

By and large, those who have transformed their learning functions have done it with governing principles that are entirely consistent with Lean but Agile. Accenture, a global management consulting, technology services, and outsourcing company, is an apt example. A book written about Accenture in 2006 (well in advance of the far worse economic meltdown in 2008) reports:[9]

> Over the past several years, Accenture has experienced a dramatic transformation, spurred by one of the most challenging times in Accenture's history—indeed, in the history of the global economy. Faced with worldwide economic turmoil . . . the broad effects of global terrorism, the rapidly changing needs of corporations and governments—our clients—and increased margin pressures, the traditional field of "training" appeared to be a relic of a different era. The rules of the training game had changed— and changed permanently.

Perhaps it is not surprising that change in learning would come earlier in Accenture's organization-transformation process than would other organizational functions, even though Accenture's learning function has been widely recognized and lauded by the external training community. Learning leadership at Accenture saw the need to make these changes:

■   To be viable, enterprise-learning programs now must meet the strategic needs of the organization. That the learning program is "important" can no longer be the justification for learning.

■   Besides its impact on consultant billing rates and performance, learning may also serve strategic needs by a positive impact on recruiting and retention.

■   It is no longer acceptable to run learning as a cost center. Learning must be run with one eye on the value being created and another on the costs.

■   Training that is planned by the centralized organization is still a component, but the learning agenda is also identified by workers. Both self-directed and directed learning efforts are important.

An award-winning study showed that Accenture's transformed learning function was producing $4.53 of value to its bottom line for every $1.00 invested in learning, a 353 percent return on learning. At the same time, through learning efficiencies instituted over a five-year period, Accenture was able to reduce spending on learning by more than 40 percent, despite a 50 percent growth in employees during this period. What Lean but Agile company would not want to report results like these?

Accenture exemplifies many principles that drive the Lean but Agile learning practices we recommend next, including focus on strategic work, cost-effective leveraging of resources, and the tailoring of learning practices to individual needs. *Flexibility* to respond quickly and change directions without orphaning previous efforts is another important aspect.

1. *Employee development is an investment, not an entitlement.* It is easy to commit to the platitude that learning and development is good, and more is better. Organizations may pride themselves on providing workers with an average of two weeks of training per year, with every employee receiving a minimum of one week. However, a review of research on corporate training transfer shows that material covered in traditional classroom training is retained for only a few months, and much training is never applied on the job. More recently it has become widely understood that training is usually *not the solution* to performance issues, although it may be one important component. Looking at worker development as an *investment* can vastly affect practices. Start to ask whether development is a good investment, or even better, what development opportunities are the best investments. An investment in employee development should withstand comparison with alternative investments, say in hardware or advertising. Development should be used *selectively and strategically*. Incumbents of jobs that have been identified as core to the organization may justify greater investment. ROI analysis (see below) is one good way to select between many alternatives. Two weeks of guaranteed development per year, although a nice luxury, may not be a luxury that the Lean but Agile organization can afford. Like a vacation, it may be wonderful while in progress, but the impact may be short-lived.

2. *Forecast ROI on employee development.* Earlier we mentioned that Accenture *evaluated* its ROI on employee development in 2006 and calculated that it was plus 353 percent. It is also possible to *forecast* employee development ROI before development occurs. Investments in talent management can be very large, particularly for leadership and management-development programs. The cost of development includes direct costs of training and

training administration and, even more significant, compensation costs of the participants and lost productivity during the training program.

ROI forecasting identifies the development that will maximize the payback from limited training resources *before* time and money are spent. It is also a tool to reduce the complexities of choosing from literally thousands of alternate development investments. For example, is development that addresses one critical need better than development that is more expensive but addresses two? What is more important, the competency gap that affects the most workers, or the gap that affects the most critical workers? It may also be useful when forecasting ROI to consider the level of certainty we have that today's development need will still be present tomorrow when the development is complete.

3. *Avoid wasteful approaches to employee development.* Some of the more common and wasteful learning and development approaches include:

- *The Tidal Wave:* Flooding the same training over the entire organization.

- *The Forced March:* Everyone follows a preset, inflexible sequence of development.

- *The Grocery Store:* Employees choose courses from the organization development resource guide but without assessments that would help determine what development will best meet organizational needs.

4. *JIT reduces the unpredictability of training.* Just-in-time training (JITT) lessens loss of training investments due to changing needs or workers walking away. Although succession planners may be comforted when they see a deep bench of highly proficient candidates, it may come at a high cost. It is not necessary to have talent 100 percent ready today for a future assignment. It may actually be more desirable to aim for a mix of *developed* and *developing*, for example, one backup that is fully developed, and others one to two years way. Having talent ready too early can result in additional compensation costs as well as higher turnover as prepared individuals leave the organization for another where they can immediately apply their talents.

JITT can be implemented in a number of ways:

a. When general and technical training are needed, first provide general training that applies to many jobs to make it easier to place people where they are needed. For example, research conducted by ACT WorkKeys has identified high-performance workforce competencies that are valuable for any education level and skilled or professional occupations (see Figure 6-1).[10]

Figure 6-1: ACT WorkKeys Work Readiness System

Competencies	Competency Groups
• Applied Mathematics • Locating Information • Reading for Information	National Career Readiness Certificate
• Applied Technology • Business Writing • Listening • Teamwork • Workplace Observation • Writing	Other Foundational Competencies
• Fit • Performance • Talent	Soft Skills

It is not difficult to forecast training duration. If new equipment will be in place in six months and training requires one month, it is best to hold off on training until month four or five. This ensures that business or environmental changes will not negate the importance of the skill set (if, for example, the equipment will not be ready for use on schedule) and lessens the chance that the worker will be recruited by another organization after the training investment has been made. If the training is too involved to wait until the last moment, do some of the training JIT, so that if the individual leaves, less of an investment is made.

b. Train smaller, more frequent groups of workers, but bigger groups for class-type development where quantity has cost efficiencies (it does not pay to provide a traditional class to a small audience). For example, rather than training one hundred engineers all at once in a new technology, it may make sense to split the engineers into four groups and ensure that the competency need develops as expected.

c. Be prepared to assign newly trained workers to work that utilizes their new skill sets as quickly as possible to gain a larger return on the investment and reduce the probability that the workers may leave.

5. *Speed processing through the development pipeline.* Challenges in contemporary talent management are analogous to operations problems that were analyzed years ago. Internal training is like a supply chain. The goal is to speed processing time and reduce bottlenecks. Internal development began to lose favor beginning in the 1970s and 1980s, in part because development times were too long. In other words, it might take ten years to develop an individual into a manager, and by then demand changes. For example, even a relatively small 3 percent overestimate per year of demand would in ten years result in a 30 percent glut.

Developing people faster means there will be more time to benefit. Here are a few strategies to speed development:[11]

■ Shorten development assignments. Research has shown that during eighteen-month internships, 80 percent of learning takes place during the first 20 percent (three and a half months) of the job assignment. Internships might be limited to four months and then reassessed to determine if there is benefit in continuing.

■ Limit development to regular bottleneck capacity. If only a limited number of developmental positions exist, do not have more people in development than can fit through the bottleneck, or figure out a way to reduce the bottleneck, such as by developing some people in assignments outside the organization.

■ Reduce developmental assignments that must be experienced in a particular order.

6. *Meet multiple development needs with each developmental activity.* Try to find developmental assignments that combine broader learning in one assignment. For example, one developmental assignment might teach both marketing and finance. This increases learning ROI and can also reduce queuing issues caused by too few developmental job assignments.

7. *Hire internally.* Using the internal talent pool for the highest possible percentage of hires was mentioned twice previously because of its positive

effect on hiring and on retention, but it is equally important for maintaining both organizational and individual incentives to engage in internal development.

8. *Craft the proper mix of internal and external development resources.* A worker-development function requires infrastructure including learning specialists and administrative staff, development resources, and technology to aid in administration and delivery of development. If local schools are not successfully educating students, even more burden may be placed on companies to educate their workforce. Particularly for smaller organizations, the per capita infrastructure costs of learning and development may be high.

Virtually every organization already employs a mix of internal and external development resources. Even when doing internal development, it is common to use external resources, such as outside providers of e-learning content. What elements of development are best done internally versus externally? Here are some of the considerations:

- What kinds of internal development are feasible for us? On-the-job? E-learning? Classroom training?

- Do we have a track record of being able to retain the persons we develop?

- Is employee development a competitive advantage for us?

- What types of skills are unique to our organization? These probably require internal development.

- What development resources (community colleges, technical schools, employer associations, etc.) are available locally?

- Can we partner with the L&D functions of any other organizations?

9. *Let other organizations develop your talent.* Hiring developed workers is the ultimate external training strategy. This may be even more effective when you hire from your competitors. Inevitably there will be cases where you lack skill sets in your talent pool and where there will be insufficient time to develop skills internally, especially in highly competitive industries where changes in products and strategies are rapid and product-development cycles are measured in months, not years. There may be wholesale changes in technology that require workers who have been developed else-

where. For example, to the extent that new drugs are developed using biotechnology, companies with physical chemists may need to look outside.

10. *Cross-training may pay off.* Cross-training leads to greater agility particularly because it allows staffing alternatives in situations of talent undersupply or oversupply. It can also reduce the chance of losing valuable talent. Cross-training is discussed further in Case Study 2, Brownells.

11. *On-the-job training (OJT) is Lean but Agile.* Increasingly, employee development is OJT, not in the classroom. The widely discussed "70-20-10 rule" states that 70 percent of development should be done on the job; 20 percent of competencies should be developed through networking with associates, in-person or through social media; and 10 percent of development should be made up of formal training.

Different training modalities are often best combined. For example, training in budgeting might begin in a classroom setting and then be followed by an assignment to help develop the department budget with the coaching of the manager. Additionally, the manager might identify experienced, competent budget developers and suggest that trainees approach these people for advice.

During OJT, individuals continue working and producing a financial return for the organization. Depth of initial learning and learning retention may be greater because learners are usually very motivated to develop the skills they need to survive the day. Further, they retain and understand how to use skills they have practiced on the job. Contrast this with sending an employee to an external management institute that has a high initial price tag, takes the employee away from work, and may result in networking that leads to the individual going to work for another organization.

With the advent of widespread competency modeling, many more jobs can be used for development purposes because the relationship between different jobs is clearer.

12. *Consider job rotations outside your organization.* Job rotations are a tried-and-true method of developing learners. Rotations have been used successfully for many types of development, from management trainees to physicians. Lean but Agile organizations may want to consider the potential of *external* rotations both for development and for development role scalability. We have discussed the steep learning curves for individuals during the

first three to four months of development assignments, and this may be even greater in another organization.

External rotations might be selected at times of lower workload. For example, Australian accounting firms provide their staffs with rotations in U.S. accounting firms during Australia's slow season, which corresponds with the busy season of American accounting firms (see chapter 3). The American firms pick up the compensation of the Australian secondees during this period.

13. *Certification programs help ensure results from development.* Competency assessments can be made in many ways, such as by tests, observation, supervisor or multirater feedback, assessment centers, behavioral interviews, or role plays. The development of competency assessments can be quite time-consuming and expensive, and an organization can easily have hundreds of important competencies. Therefore, a preponderance of organizational competency assessments use simple rating instruments that are completed by oneself, a supervisor, and sometimes colleagues. These types of assessments, however, are subject to many common rater errors (for example, halo or leniency) and their accuracy is often suspect.

Certifications are a more reliable indicator that an individual has achieved a prescribed level of knowledge and/or skill. Certification programs typically involve two components: training or materials on a comprehensive, carefully selected body of knowledge; and a professionally developed, valid, and reliable test of knowledge or skill acquisition. Professional certifications are designed to comply with high standards set by organizations such as the American National Standards Institute (ANSI) or the Institute for Credentialing Excellence (ICE), which accredit the certifications of other organizations. Industry certifications are developed by organizations that represent various professions (for example, the American Society of Training and Development) as well as organizations that see a benefit of certifying users of their products, for example, Microsoft Corporation. There are certifications for public accountants, financial planners, human resources specialists, auto mechanics, IT specialists, and many more professions.

Although many certifications are available in the public domain, they commonly are available only for a small percentage of the roles within most organizations. Increasingly, companies see benefit in developing internal certifications just for their own workforces. These internally developed certifications share many of the characteristics of industry-wide certifications. A careful analysis is done to identify the necessary knowledge and skills and one or several reliable assessment techniques are used to verify knowledge acquisition.

Certifications provide confidence that individuals can perform tasks that are central to standard jobs with high proficiency. Because of the consistency and reliability of certifications, they simplify the process of moving people within or between roles. Certified individuals can typically operate with equal effectiveness in their local work setting or when they move across the globe. To date, millions of certifications have been issued—even more than academic degrees. Helping workers get certified may often be a better investment than tuition reimbursement for an academic degree.

14. *Leverage technology.* Technology has a rapidly increasing role in learning. Even e-learning, one of the more mature and pervasive technologies, continues to evolve in effectiveness as the quality of offerings improves and more workers are comfortable with technology-brokered training increases. Besides its use for learning delivery, technology is becoming increasingly critical for learning development, learning management, and collaborative learning (the "20" in the 70-20-10 approach). Technology improves ROI by increasing development benefits and reducing costs. Use technology to:

- Reduce the high costs of traditional training, including facilities and travel costs.
- Rapidly create high-quality learning content.
- Provide learning on demand, twenty-four/seven, globally.
- Facilitate social learning, communities of practice, and coaching.
- Manage and disseminate bodies of knowledge.
- More easily test learning comprehension.
- Help workers learn and grow almost every day, rather than confining learning to a few days or weeks of formal training.

15. *Have workers help fund their own development.* Workers who receive development may receive increased compensation, broader employability, and intrinsic benefits such as more interesting or impactful work. Additionally, short tenure means that workers often benefit more from their devel-

opment than their organizations do. Should employees help finance their learning, much like their college degrees, especially for voluntary training? Many CWs already bear the primary burden for their education and may be willing to help pay for training they receive from an organization that uses them. Some organizations might invite potential workers to training before work begins without salary or at a training rate that is lower than the rate of a trained worker.

EMs may contribute to their development costs other than by paying tuition. They can engage in development on their own time, whether that means taking training after hours or on weekends or volunteering for development roles while continuing to do their regular jobs. Some organizations can use training as a profit center through internal billing or by opening training to workers outside the organization.

16. *Offer development opportunities for interns.* Internships can be a wonderful development opportunity, particularly for students. Internships help students determine what work is a good fit and provide a leg up in being selected later by employers. A carefully structured internship benefits the organization by providing low-cost assistance, a good way to find talented individuals, and an opportunity to contribute to the community at large.

Some individuals now pay for internships, so internships can be revenue neutral or positive. Having interns pay for their internship may strike some as unjust or confiscatory. But internships present learning opportunities that may well be more effective than much more costly college classroom training.

17. *Support dual career paths.* "Dual career paths" enable individuals to advance in compensation and rank through successively higher management positions or through their own technical specialties. This helps organizations benefit from the technical contributions of individuals who have been developed for many years at considerable cost and whose replacement would be costly.

18. *A time for development within position.* Lean organizations tend to be flatter organizations, and there are fewer positions to which one can advance. For that reason, "development within position" is often the most viable option. Workers naturally will want increased compensation commensurate with new skills and responsibilities, and broad-banding has been suggested. Compensation budget limits have at least in part prevented broad-banding from achieving its expected potential. More flexible job descriptions, however,

should allow individuals to contribute more and reduce hesitation to pay significantly more while they hold the same position.

19. *Development investments before a merger or an acquisition may be wasted.* Mergers and acquisitions (M&As) or other sources of instability do not mesh well with L&D programs. During these periods, a temporary hiatus may be appropriate.

M&As frequently lead to downsizing to reduce duplicate talent as well as increased voluntary turnover. Talent that has been developed at considerable expense is usually lost. Restructuring is likely, and career ladders may be broken. An acquiring company often divests parts of the business to reduce debt, which leads to more turmoil. Despite common assurances that it is "business as usual," workers and supervisors know better and will not be fully engaged in new learning. Therefore, the strategy should be clarified and workforce plans should be revisited prior to ramping up training after a major organizational change.

20. *It may be time to reduce the role of supervisors in training and development.* Once upon a time, workers participated in a "forced march" of development activities that were orchestrated and owned by the organization. Today workers are often required to take an active role in initiating development, particularly career development that prepares them for new roles.

Traditionally supervisors have been told they share responsibility for employee development, but it is an area where most supervisors perennially fail to perform well. It is not difficult to imagine why. Other than providing sufficient training for a worker to do his or her current work, a supervisor rarely has an incentive (or the skills) to do more. Training takes needed resources away from work and lowers productivity. It may result in valued employees going to other internal functions or leaving the organization altogether. Supervisors naturally balk at additional administrative burdens. Even supervisors who are inclined to support career development do not know how and/or have not been provided with the necessary tools to do it well.

Conceivably, supervisors are more motivated to participate in development assignments for persons who are not direct reports because in the process they may receive additional resources. Ultimately, it may make more sense to let career development responsibility rest with individual workers and to provide them with supporting tools and career development specialists with central vision and development expertise.

21. *Create strong links of development with all other aspects of talent management.* Integrated talent management unites formerly disparate functions like employee selection, employee development, performance management, and succession planning around common goals and shared competency models. The linkages allow all the programs to be more impactful as well as more efficient. Worker development should not be a stand-alone venture. Integrating it with other talent functions is one of the surest ways to increase its value. The same holds true for all other talent-management functions.

Performance Planning and Review

It is difficult to conceive of an area of worker management subject to more brickbats than performance reviews. Performance planning and review systems are such an easy target that even the cartoon character Dilbert[12] has repeatedly raised legitimate criticisms, and comedian John Cleese has hilariously lampooned performance reviews for years. Many organizations have failed to gain value from them, yet they proceed anyway because reviews are traditional, required, or thought to be necessary to defend employee actions such as involuntary terminations. At a recent meeting, one of the authors sat with a vice president of human resources and three HR managers and heard them all speak about the uselessness of their performance review system. When we suggested that maybe it should be sacked, the VP was receptive, but the HR managers were appalled and adamant that the practice could not possibly be dropped. However, some pioneering firms have decided that they are not going to do them anymore (see Case Study 2, Brownells).

Our view is that it is high time for organizations to drop performance review programs *if* they are not producing demonstrable value. Thousands of articles (including some by the authors) have been written on how to redesign performance reviews to gain benefit, but they all presuppose that an organization is *willing* and *able* to do what it takes, whether it is clear goal setting, supervisor coaching, managing rater error, or substantial rewarding of good performance. If performance reviews are ended, it is important to institute other approaches that provide individuals with a clear vision of mission and work priorities as well as feedback and coaching to continually grow. Performance history, which is critical for managing the talent pool effectively, can also be captured in other ways. For example, one might examine the work history of an individual and see that he managed five audits to the satisfaction of the client.

While some Lean but Agile organizations may find it is best to stop performance reviews, at least for a time, others will benefit from expanding their use. When work is divided into projects, an end-of-project review is common. Agile teams (described earlier) have reviews at the end of every cycle, as frequently as every two weeks. In short, the key to successfully navigating the shoals of performance management is doing an objective evaluation and determining how it can best add value in your organization. Lean but Agile suggestions for performance planning and review follow.

1. *What's sauce for the goose is sauce for the gander.* Elements of performance planning and review systems for employees could be beneficially applied to contractors, and elements of contractor performance management could be beneficially applied to employees.

Organizations tend to set much higher standards for performance planning for CWs than they do for employees. Consider the typical performance plan that a consultant must create to be considered for work:

- *Overview of the Work:* The consultant must demonstrate an understanding of the high-level goals of the work, the intended benefits, and the conditions that may affect the work.

- *Background of the Consultant or Team:* This establishes that the consultant has the needed capabilities and experience to be successful.

- *The Deliverables:* Outcomes and results that will be achieved are described in detail.

- *Methodology:* The consultant recommends the best way to get the work done.

- *Project Plan and Timeline:* This details each step and the expected time to complete the work.

- *Pricing:* The consultant must identify the resources that will be required to complete the work.

A good performance plan provides a clear vision of what is expected as well as an agreed path—a map of how to get there. Employees, in contrast to consultants, often have no performance plan, and when they do, most have scant detail. Having a clear view of the deliverables is most important, followed closely by an agreed plan to get there, regardless of who creates the plan. Most employees, when asked, indicate that "outstanding" has never been defined for them, which raises a serious concern. *How is it that employees can be implored to be outstanding, but that most often no one has bothered to define for them what outstanding means and how it is measurably and objectively defined?*

Developing proposals or performance plans can be very tedious, but sometimes there are shortcuts. If work is repetitive, then common performance standards for everyone in the same role will serve to define expectations and best practices used by successful performers. If an individual's work is varying and project-based, then a plan that contains the elements of a consultant's proposal would be beneficial. It is not beyond the realm of reason to have employees or teams bid for work and to have the merits of their bids compared to those of CWs.

Consultants and other contractors, in contrast to employees, often do not receive performance reviews, and records are seldom kept of how they did. If a proposal exists, a consultant evaluation may be a simple matter of rating the contractor on the deliverables and whether the project was delivered on time and on budget. Multirater assessments that include all the persons who have worked with the consultant might also provide valuable performance history.

Each contractor, like each employee, requires investment and becomes more valuable to the organization over time with greater organizational knowledge and experience. The ROI of the investment can be increased by using effective contractors repeatedly. If systems are already in place for conducting employee reviews, why not also use them for contractor reviews?

2. *Review your goal-setting process.* Many organizations have implemented forms of management by objectives (MBO). MBO seeks to ensure that work is tied directly to organization objectives, called *linkage*. In the most recent incarnation of MBO, the organization's objectives are established based on a balanced scorecard and are then cascaded down through key performance indicators (KPIs) and behaviors linked to successful demonstrations of competencies. In larger and more hierarchical organizations, the process can take months of effort to follow a systematic process of

developing goals at each level and then cascading them down to each successive level. Sometimes work is delayed until the new plan is finalized.

After plans are established, there may be slavish adherence to them, even when changing circumstances suggest other courses of action. Incorrect business forecasts and plans can lead to a loss of faith. Given all these factors, could it be that less time should be spent on planning and more time on recognizing and adapting to changes? One size does not fit all. Organizations with predictable funding and workflow may find that traditional planning approaches still work fine. For those organizations with a more fluid environment, it makes sense to consider whether a planning process advocated in 1954 by Peter Drucker[13] to meet very different conditions needs to be streamlined to better meet the needs of the twenty-first century.

3. *Invest more development in workers with good reviews.* Employee development is a component of many performance-planning processes. Individuals with more pronounced deficits are more likely to have a development plan, and plans generally focus on performance gaps. Conceivably there would be greater benefit in focusing development on exemplary performers and enhancing their strengths. We have recommended that rigid job descriptions be jettisoned in favor of individual role descriptions, a unique set of duties that maximize the contributions of an individual's strengths. With more flexible assignments, correcting deficits becomes less important, and focusing attention on strong performers is likely to increase their tenure. This is not to suggest that a mediocre performer should not receive coaching to improve performance. But why wait until review time to do that? Instead, performance review time might be an opportune time to plan the next assignment.

4. *Do performance reviews when needed, not based on a rigid schedule.* Performance reviews are appropriate when a project is finished or when parties agree that discussion is warranted. Although certain processes—for example, bonus pay—may be facilitated by requiring performance reviews for all employees at the same time, would worker recognition and thanks be sufficient in many instances? Why not let supervisors and/or employees ask for performance reviews as needed?

5. *Not all performance reviews require supervisor input.* Individuals generally have more information about their work and its outcomes than anyone else. It may be appropriate, particularly with interim reviews during projects, to use self-reviews and possibly multirater reviews.

6. *Cumulative performance reviews are more accurate.* Lean but Agile management requires informative, reliable performance history, but performance ratings often vary due to factors unrelated to actual performance. For example, supervisors in organizations with fixed rating distributions often feel they need to evenly distribute the limited number of high ratings they give each year. If an individual received one of the valuable, quota-limited top ratings last year, she will not this year, even if performance is better. Performance ratings can vary when a new supervisor takes over; she may be more lenient or stricter than her predecessor. Common rater errors often apply.

Cumulative performance reviews are a reasonable alternative to improving validity and reliability. We recommend a weighted average of performance reviews over the time a person has worked for the organization. Since these reviews are based on a longer history of performance, they are more likely to be reliable indicators of a person's contribution. This is similar to the notion of GPA—grade-point average—which looks at the cumulative performance of a student.

More recent performance reviews are a better predictor of future performance than reviews that were done long ago when the work and other circumstances affecting the individual may have differed. It makes sense to give a heavier weighting to more recent reviews. For example, the performance rating might be an average computed for up to the past ten years, with the present year given full weight, last year's review multiplied by 0.9, the previous by 0.8, and so forth.

Succession Planning

Succession planning, even more so than other talent-management practices, must change to respond better to the speed of change and uncertainty of the business environment. Restructurings, downsizing, mergers, and acquisitions all change organizational structures and negate the benefits of succession plans. Shorter employee tenures often mean that backup charts are out of date well before their annual updates. The answer to one simple question can tell a lot about a succession-planning program: *How many positions are filled based on succession-planning charts? Alternatively, how often are succession charts even consulted when openings occur? How long does it take to fill positions, and what percentage of filled positions result in at least satisfactory or superior performance?*

Traditionally, leadership continuity has been the primary objective of succession planning. Toward this end, it is common for succession-planning programs to identify a (relatively) small number of critical positions, often the top several layers of the organization and/or divisions, and develop a short roster of backups for each. Some charts are populated by job incumbents who, working alone, are asked to indicate which of their direct reports could fill in for them. Other organizations conduct talent reviews of job incumbents in the top layers of the organization once a year. Individuals may be rated as having *potential* to move up in the organization, as well-placed in the current position, or as possibly not being a fit to continue in the organization. More so than the often hastily assembled backup rosters or subjective measures of potential, careful reviews of individual development needs can provide real value.

If performance planning is the most criticized talent-management practice, succession planning is probably the most subjective. (It does not have to be, but it often is.) Most succession talent reviews can be characterized as light on data and heavy on opinion. We have already discussed at length (see chapter 3) the many issues associated with measuring a construct as fuzzy as individual *potential.*

Candidate performance is also typically evaluated during talent reviews, a more appropriate measure in our opinion than potential. Some organizations use organizational performance reviews. Other organizations acknowledge that their performance reviews do not provide reliable data for succession planning and instead make a separate performance rating, which also may be very subjective due to a lack of clear performance criteria.

Instead, candidates could be measured on their competency match with job requirements, detailed performance history, and the match of their personal preferences with job characteristics such as job structure, teamwork, decision making, etc. In other words, we recommend matching both on capability to do the job and on personal fit/preference for the work.

Succession planning interfaces well with an organization talent pool. Both seek to identify talent in advance of a need. A company talent pool, however, covers more positions, uses more and better candidate data, and is updated more frequently. An organization with a mature talent pool based on the recommended five talent indicators—(1) performance history, (2) competence, (3) education, (4) experience, and (5) personal preferences/fit—has already done much of the heavy lifting required to do objective succession planning.

Succession planning *extends* the work by creating a miniature talent pool of prime suspects *and* proactively manages their development to better ensure good candidates. Here are some suggestions for Lean but Agile succession planning.

1. *Be strategic and selective with succession planning.*[14] Like all practices in lean organizations, the logic and ROI of doing succession planning should be reviewed, not blindly accepted. A robotically developed, poorly conceived succession plan is a waste of valuable resources and is worse than none. It may be common practice to create succession plans for positions from the top one to three levels in the organization, but it is unlikely that there is equivalent need for succession for every position. On the other hand, there are most likely positions below the top three levels that should have succession plans. Prioritize by considering these criteria and others that may be important to your organization:

- How difficult would it be to fill the role from the outside?
- How much development or startup time would a likely successor need?
- How important is it to fill the role immediately? How damaging would it be if it remained open for a while?
- How likely is it that current incumbents might turn over soon?

The organization's size can impact the design of succession planning. Some organizations may achieve a more appropriate scale by creating pools or succession charts that service the needs of multiple divisions and take advantage of the portfolio principle that we discussed earlier. Although definitely unconventional, some smaller organizations could achieve economies of scale by sharing succession pools with other organizations, or even by "trading" talented individuals, much as is currently done in professional sports.

2. *"Hire from outside" or "deal with it when necessary" are valid succession plans.* Even when it is clear that succession should be planned, it does not necessarily follow that the best succession approach is to develop a bench of current employees. Alternatively, it might be better to fill the backup chart with talent pool members, to plan to hire from the outside, or even to defer the decision until the need arises. The degree of fit of potential

internal backups, the capability of the organization to make a succession plan and develop individuals effectively, and the availability of candidates outside the organization are all important considerations. The "chain of moves" problem is another consideration, especially in lean organizations. Filling a job internally usually creates a new gap, and filling that second gap creates still another that must be filled with an effective replacement. Does it make sense to populate a replacement chart with internal candidates who are a poor match with the role requirements? Probably not.

3. *Consider succession pools and developing candidates with a broad set of competencies.* Are succession replacement charts still viable today for filling vacant roles? Some consultants have recommended that succession be made more agile by replacing multiple job replacement charts with a smaller number of succession pools. A *succession pool* provides backups for a group of jobs, for example, all executive jobs. The list of candidates in a pool tends to be larger than in a replacement chart, which lessens the problems associated with candidates being no longer available and/or roles requiring new skill sets that the backups may not have. The combination of more candidates and more jobs provides infinitely more options.

If succession pools are used instead of replacement charts, then it makes sense to evaluate and develop candidates on a broader set of competencies to qualify them for a broader array of positions. Succession pools may also be beneficial in ameliorating false expectations created when an individual is on a very short list of candidates for one position.

4. *Update competency models during talent reviews.* Role requirements become out of date quickly. Talent review time is ideal for tweaking role competency models. Job incumbents' successes and challenges are indicative of what it takes to be successful in the position. If role requirements are not updated during talent reviews when the necessary data are available, then when?

5. *Measure bench strength in functional areas and critical competencies.* It is common (and valuable) to measure the strength of backups for a role. For example, proficiency of candidates might be measured on a scale from 1 (low) to 100 (high). An average proficiency of *85* for backups for the CEO would indicate greater bench strength than an average backup strength of *50* for the CFO.

To get more stable and useful bench strength measures, we recommend that bench strength be measured for functional areas (for example, finance) and/or for particularly critical competencies. These are more likely to give a meaningful, big-picture view of backup strengths and areas of threat, and they are statistically more reliable because they are based on larger numbers of candidates.

6. *Schedule more frequent talent reviews.* Admittedly, convening all the necessary parties and taking them away from work to do talent reviews is costly; once a year may already seem challenging. Still there is good reason to question whether once a year is frequent enough. As already noted, *annual* succession plans are often disconnected from the immediacy of *daily* business decisions. Further, agile organizations are shortening worker development cycles; three to four months may provide 80 percent of the value of eighteen-month development assignments. Quarterly mini talent reviews between individuals and qualified coaches or T&D professionals are an alternative that will help ensure that individual learning is still on track and that development resources are being used wisely.

7. *Reshuffle the deck.* Succession plans are traditionally designed to help organizations fill critical positions when an individual is either reassigned or leaves the organization. Alternatively, especially in Lean but Agile organizations, the departure of an individual may be the time to reorganize and reassign roles. Is it necessary that a backup perform the exact same duties as her predecessor, given that her strengths and weaknesses are not identical? A set of roles formerly assigned to one individual may be divided differently and potentially reassigned to three or four persons. Lean but Agile organizations are well-armed to reshuffle roles when an individual leaves because the process is the same as the one used to optimize work or project assignments.

Lean Calculations

Most talent-management decisions result in benefits as well as costs, but often the net value of different decisions is far from intuitive. Although the net economic value of a talent-management decision may not always be the deciding factor, it is particularly important in a lean organization to understand economic impacts of different decisions. We have already recommended ROI analyses, for example, when evaluating employee development alternatives.

Rough estimates are better than none. You do not necessarily need to employ complex modeling or operations research methods.

For example, suppose we are considering two candidates for a position. Should we select the worker with five years of experience or the worker with one year? The more experienced individual would require a 20 percent higher salary. *If* five years of experience translates into greater competence, then it clearly has value. In general, the value of experience depends both on the time it takes to become proficient in a particular job and on the learning agility of an individual. A person with twenty years of experience may be no more competent than one with five years, but a person with three years of experience might be far better than an individual with just one year.

We might quantify experience by considering the *readiness* of an individual to contribute today at a high level. We might calculate how much of a salary premium would be justified for a person who is 100 percent proficient, or whether a resource who is ready today is ultimately a better buy than one who can be ready in six months. Sample calculations are shown in Figure 6-2.

Figure 6-2: Calculation of the Relative Merit of Selecting Resource 1 or 2

1. Resource 1 (R1) is fully proficient immediately, is paid $50,000 per year, and produces $150,000 per year for 2.5 years, a gross contribution of $375,000. Subtracting R1's salary for 2.5 years, $125,000, the net contribution is $250,000 over 2.5 years.
2. Resource 2 (R2) is less developed than R1 and is paid an average of $40,000 per year. R2 averages about 75 percent proficiency for 6 months (worth $56,250), and then 100 percent proficiency, $150,000 per year, for the next two years, or $300,000, a gross contribution of $356,250. Subtracting R2's salary for 2.5 years, $100,000, from the total contribution leaves a net of $256,250, slightly more than R1's net contribution.

Notes:
   a) If we have expended resources to develop R2, these would need to be subtracted from R2's net contribution, which could make R1 a better choice.
   b) We could try to increase the net value of R2 by accelerating her development and cutting the time it takes R2 to reach full proficiency to 3 months.
   c) This sample calculation shows a very small difference between the net contributions of R1 and R2, but in many cases a calculation such as this will help save far larger sums, potentially millions of dollars.

Chapter Summary

This chapter reviewed three key Lean but Agile principles: (1) focus on strategic, high-impact work; (2) build a talent pool; and (3) use alternative workers. The chapter then examined the implications of Lean but Agile for people management practices, including staffing, retention, learning and development, performance management, and succession planning.

CHAPTER 7

BRING LEAN BUT AGILE WORK AND WORKFORCE PLANNING INTO YOUR ORGANIZATION

NOW LET'S EXAMINE the key elements for incorporating the planning and implementing of Lean but Agile work and workforce planning into your organization. This chapter focuses on building commitment to Lean but Agile work and workforce planning by making the business case; focusing on outcomes; setting relevant benchmarks; changing management and communication strategies; determining key stakeholders, roles, and accountabilities; establishing strategies; setting timelines; and using technology as a tool for introducing Lean but Agile work and workforce planning into your organization.

Building a Commitment to Lean but Agile

Throughout this book we have stressed the need to focus on the outcomes and objectives of the organization in any human capital activity. In introducing *Lean but Agile work and workforce planning* principles to your organization, it is imperative that the same focus be applied to the creation of a business case and implementation strategy (the project). Consider: *What is the targeted outcome of the project? How does that outcome link explicitly to the organizational objectives?*

These are key questions. The answers will form the foundation of a strategy to make a compelling business case for the incremental introduction of Lean but Agile work and workforce planning into an organization.

Making the Business Case by Focusing on Outcomes

Too often significant human capital initiatives fail to gain traction with senior leaders. There may be myriad reasons for this lack of interest. The authors, over many years of consulting, recognize a common theme in the responses that senior leaders give when they are asked why they rejected various human capital proposals: the skepticism of leaders that such initiatives have any real value (value for money) to improve bottom-line performance.

Leaders quite often tell us that human capital programs are "nice to have" in the good times. But those programs are often first cut in the bad times. We have explained in chapter 2 that the key reason for this skepticism is the human resources focus on *outputs* rather than on *outcomes*. Human resources, as a department, does not consistently link the desired business outcome to the human resources activity that precedes that outcome.

How then can we change leadership opinion about the bottom-line financial value of human capital programs?

The surest way to prove the value of a Lean but Agile work and workforce planning program and related projects is to link their outcomes to organizational objectives. Leaders must have a clear "line of sight" between talent-management activities and desired organizational objectives. Organizations need to understand the impact the human capital drivers have on outcomes and organizational objectives.

Many human capital reporting tools are available for this purpose. Most large Human Resource Information Systems (HRIS) solutions have reporting capability. Whether these reports are linked to the organization's objectives is under question. As mentioned in an earlier chapter, linking all assessments of human capital drivers to the organizational objectives will support the Lean but Agile work and workforce planning program and provide conclusive evidence of the value of these programs in the terms leadership understands, and, in turn, will focus on.

The recent concentration on creating human resources standards and defensible ways to repeatedly measure them, which have been featured in chapter 2, has also led to further development on a range of human capital measures.

Example 7-1: Human Capital Indices Reporting

One recently developed tool for reporting on organizational goals and objectives is the Sonar Vision on Demand (SVOD) from OrcaEyes.[1] The reports generated by this tool cover a broad cross-section of human capital drivers and focus on potential risks, which include:

Financial Risk
- Overtime risk
- Revenue risk
- Sales revenue risk

Overtime Risk
- Surplus payroll risk
- Time to fill impacting overtime, earnings
- Training costs to earnings
- Premium costs to earnings
- Premium costs to profit

Operational Risk
- Projects
- Productivity per employee
- Overtime levels to accidents
- Leave to accidents
- Employee engagement
- Manager satisfaction

Strategic Plan Risk
- Individual components
- Critical projects
- Major contracts

Workforce Planning and Organizational Readiness Risk
- Employee gap to employee surplus
- Turnover—overall
- Turnover—voluntary
- Turnover—involuntary
- Turnover—monthly
- Performance turnover
- Fill rate

- Fill rate—external
- Fill rate—internal
- Fill rate—employee type
- Fill rate—part-time/full-time
- Time to fill

Top Performer Loss Risk
- Performance turnover
- Flight risk—below average pay
- Performance retirement

Head Count and Compensation Risk
- Head count to budget
- Full-time equivalent (FTE) head count to budget
- Contractor temp head count
- Span of control
- Compensation fully loaded
- Salary
- Overtime
- Contractor temp
- Temp costs to earnings
- Earnings per employee
- Earnings per dollar spent

Aging Demographic Risk
- Retirement—overall
- Retirement to tenure
- Average age

Age Distribution, EEO, and Affirmative Action Risk
- Race distribution
- Gender distribution
- Pay discrepancy—race
- Pay discrepancy—gender

These reports focus on the impact that human capital drivers have on organizational objectives in performance to budget. Although this review is focused on the current/forecast budget period, it is a powerful example of how greater attention to human capital issues can impact bottom-line performance positively through obvious cause-and-effect reporting.

Example 7-2: Reporting on Outcome

Company Z has a major expansion planned. The human resources department is under pressure to deliver a growing number of engineers in a tightening market, staff attrition is increasing, and the percentage of staff at or near retirement age is high. This sounds like the perfect scenario for a failed recruitment drive.

As in most organizations, line managers were quick to blame human resources for the problems. The organization's leaders were reluctant to spend more money to support HR to deliver the desired results. Imagine the impact, however, if the business case for increased recruitment spending had been focused on loss of revenue and profit.

The latest style of analytical reporting focuses on the outcome. The screen shot in Figure 7-1 shows the positive impact (+$11,396,985) that increasing the fill rate, reducing the attrition, and postponing retirements will have for the organization, taking into account the cost of the activities. The leadership discussion immediately focused on how quickly the programs could be initiated.

Figure 7-1: Reporting on Outcome

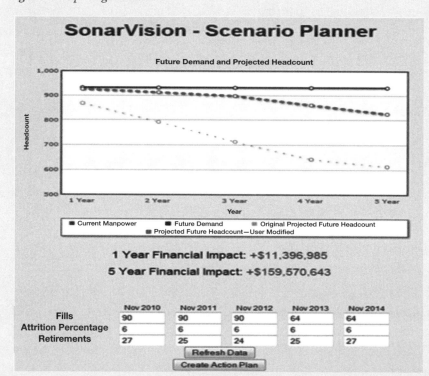

As in the example of Company Z, once the data are collected and the analyses are concluded, several causes for concern will inevitably be uncovered. A business case can be made based on these areas. The benchmarking data available through reports, such as the one in Figure 7-1, will also support the overall strategy and business case.

The reviewer will obtain an overview of potential priorities and areas of risk and impact, and from the combined analysis of future state requirements, the current state and human capital drivers.

The beauty of using something akin to human capital indices as a baseline is that the resulting reports are outcome-focused in how they represent the bottom-line impact of weaknesses and risks.

Relevant Benchmarks

Another great benefit of human capital reporting is it gives users ways to compare their organization's human capital results with industry performance. In Australasia, Asia, and the United States, plans are well-advanced to publish, by industry location and size, these types of indices. Following the publication of these indices one could ask how long it will be before investors and financial institutions start demanding this reporting on a regular basis.

Change Management and Communication Strategies

We do not intend to describe in detail the most appropriate change strategy or communication strategy. These will depend on the organization and the current environment. Traditional change management and communication strategies, if properly implemented, will deliver the required outcomes.

Key Stakeholders, Roles, and Accountabilities

Leadership support is critical for the success of Lean but Agile work and workforce planning. It is also important that communication with the project sponsor, preferably at the senior executive level within leadership, begin as soon as is practical. Making the business case should start with a review of where the organization is currently placed. To ensure support, we also recommend that the finance department and the chief financial officer (CFO) be engaged as early as possible. Having financial support for the proffered financial impacts and remedial strategies presented is crucial. In larger organizations, internal auditors may also add value by reviewing project findings.

An experienced facilitator, preferably in the role of project leader, is an important element for the program to be successful. Where possible, using the services of staff as subject matter experts also supports a strong engagement strategy.

Implementation Strategies

The implementation strategy varies by organization. Some of the criteria that may need to be considered are listed below:

- The future organization.
  - The organization's size
  - Head count
  - Physical locations
  - Companies/divisions
  - Diversity of products and/or services
- The perceived magnitude of any change. For instance, moving from a manufacturer to a marketer is a much bigger change than a slight change in product focus.
- The organizational readiness for change.
- The business cycle. Does the business work in a cyclical fashion with some periods busier than others?
- The quality of available resources for the project.

The authors believe that wherever possible, Lean but Agile programs can benefit from a pilot program. Effective pilot programs are set up to succeed by relying on a manager who strongly supports the effort for the benefits to be obtained from it and by selectively choosing participants who support the effort.

Timelines

Timelines are totally dependent on the implementation. We recommend, however, that an effective pilot program be designed for completion within six months. Our experience shows that leaders and staff sometimes have a limited attention span for projects. It is important that the pilot quickly demonstrate the positive, measurable impact it will have on delivering organizational objectives.

The outputs in the design of a *lean work/lean workforce* program for an organization would include the following:

- Clearly documented and evidenced objectives (see chapter 2)
- A clearly documented future state view (see chapter 2)
- A clearly documented and evidenced current state view (see chapter 3)
- A gap closure requirements plan (see chapter 6)
- Preparation of a clearly evidenced, supported, and funded project plan (this chapter)
- A well-founded change management and communications plan (this chapter)
- A systematic evidence-based review and realignment plan (see chapter 2)

A Note of Caution: Keeping the Program on Track

As we noted earlier in this chapter, human capital projects fail to get off the ground or falter soon after initiation. One key reason for this is the lack of focus on outcomes. Human resources activity primarily focuses on output, not on outcome. To business leaders, indicators such as average performance ratings, course completions, and head count increases do not mean much in outcomes.

Example 7-3: Process at the Cost of Outcome

Think of a typical talent-management initiative. Say an organization's leaders decide to implement a performance-management strategy to improve organizational productivity. When the program is first launched, there is normally a real understanding of why the performance-management program is important. Typically, the fanfare of a new program means everyone has an idea of why it is important. Twelve months in, however:

■ How often do we see that the focus has slipped and is more about completion of the exercise of performance management, possibly highlighting how the "score" has improved?

■ How often are the goals truly linked to the performance criteria and measured in outcomes?

■ How long does it take for the program to end up as a process, an activity trap, regarded by many people as nothing more than a time-consuming event that must be completed?

This is shown in Figure 7-2, with the lean work/lean workforce framework components as the "y" axis (input, process, output, and outcome) and time as the "x" axis.

Figure 7-2: Lean but Agile Work and Workforce Planning Framework

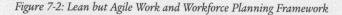

	Period 1	Period 2	Period 3
Outcome			
Output			
Process			
Input			

If there is no ongoing renewal of the link between outcome and output, then the program quickly slips into the output mode, where scores are everything, and then to the process mode, where completion is the main driver. At this point the project becomes an *activity trap* in which process is undertaken for the mere sake of the process.

It is critical with any program that there be an ongoing renewal of the linkages of the program from the objective and the targeted outcomes, and that renewal is regularly communicated throughout the organization.

Example 7-4: Focusing on Outcome, Not Output

Firm Y was presenting an overview of the successful implementation of a comprehensive talent-management solution. The implementation team was focused on results. The statistics were impressive, with performance improvement of more than 90 percent and more than 98 percent completion.

The question was asked as to what was the desired *outcome*. The response concluded that it was performance improvement at an individual level. As this appeared a little vague, *and* more an *output* than an *outcome,* further inquiry revealed that the leadership's goal was an increase in business performance across sales and customer service. The key success indicators were improved sales volumes and increased customer service ratings, resulting in improvement in the order of ten percentage points in repeat client business.

The implementation team was focused on reporting the *outputs* as proof of successful implementation. There was no linkage or reporting of *outcome,* however. The likelihood is high that this program will closely follow the outcome in Example 7-1.

Chapter Summary

This chapter presented the key elements for incorporating the planning and implementing of Lean but Agile work and workforce planning into your organization. It focused on making the business case; focusing on outcomes; setting relevant benchmarks; changing management and communication strategies; determining key stakeholders, roles, and accountabilities; establishing strategies; setting timelines; and using technology.

CHAPTER 8

THE FUTURE OF LEAN BUT AGILE WORK AND WORKFORCE PLANNING

THE MANTRA OF MODERN TIMES is that the only constant is change. As organizational leaders scramble globally to gain and sustain competitive advantage, it seems unlikely that leaders of the future will lose interest in finding ways to cut costs while improving product/service quality. Indeed, it seems that the reverse will be true.

This chapter focuses on preparing for the future of Lean but Agile work and workforce planning. It examines trends in using alternative (because different from traditional) approaches to staffing, such as outsourcing, offshoring, and insourcing. It also reviews geographical trends in staffing. Finally, the chapter offers some final frequently asked questions about Lean but Agile work and workforce planning—and their answers.

Current Trends in Using Creative Approaches to Staffing

What are the current trends in outsourcing? Offshoring? Insourcing? What trends will likely point the way to Africa as a source of future competitive talent? This section addresses these important questions.

Trends in Outsourcing

Outsourcing is commonly understood to mean moving work out of an organization to be performed in another. While cost savings can be a motivator to outsource, it is usually not the only motivator. In many cases managers believe they can get superior service from other providers rather than doing everything inside. Outsourcing is thus done occasionally to keep the focus of a business on its core (what it does best) and outsource the rest.

Much has been written about trends in outsourcing, including the outsourcing of HR. Indeed, so much has been written that it appears to be a preoccupation of many business leaders. It is easy to tell that much time and effort are being devoted to ways to move work that is not central to an organization's core to outside organizations, thought to be more efficient and effective in providing those products or services that are only peripherally related to an organization's management.

Consider just a few trends that have been identified in outsourcing:

1. Outsourcing has continued to grow even when economic conditions are not favorable for many businesses. The greatest growth has historically been in such areas as customer services, financial services, manufacturing, and information technology processing. HR outsourcing has tended to focus on areas considered "transactional," such as payroll and benefits. By outsourcing transactional work, internal HR practitioners can devote more time to such strategic initiatives as organization-wide change management, talent management, performance consulting, and ethics.

2. Outsourcing is moving from so-called back office activities such as information technology processing to more robust activities. Clients of outsourcing organizations want incremental, not transformational, changes. A major goal is to secure better quality service at reduced cost. Clients use their lucrative contracts as an incentive to enhance competition and induce outsourcing providers to do more and better work for less.

3. Organizations that outsource are finding that it does not always work best to use multiple service providers. Sometimes it is better to find one all-around provider to simplify management efforts to liaise with a provider. Multiple providers can lead to complexity and even costly, wasteful conflict.

4. Flexibility is becoming a major issue. Organizations that outsource want to sign contracts with providers for shorter periods of time. They also

want greater leeway to cut agreements short if service providers are not quickly responsive to perceived problems.

5. Some clients fight a battle between the political damage done when they outsource work out of communities and the cost savings they may derive from doing so.[1]

It may be more cost-effective to send work to lower-cost venues. But if the savings from doing that are outweighed by business loss in some locations, business leaders may think twice before they ship work—or jobs—out of a community on which they depend heavily for sales.

6. Competition among providers will grow more intense over coming years. Many organizations—and nations—would like to become outsourcing service providers. It is a growth industry. At the same time, it can give service providers an edge in negotiating additional work with the clients they serve.

7. Outsourcing providers are forming strategic alliances in bids to offer clients a broader service array. That may be particularly attractive to small providers. By striking up arrangements with noncompetitive partners, they can maintain autonomy while offering broader services or products to their clients. Of course, great care must be taken to ensure that problems caused by one provider do not lead to loss of business for all those working together in an alliance.

8. Outsourcing providers are finding that they must be sensitive to environmental issues. They must check how their organizations are managed so that they are perceived to be more environmentally friendly than their competitors. Being able to demonstrate strong environmental sensitivity provides a competitive advantage. The same is true when providers have remained sensitive to other issues that may give them competitive advantages, such as doing business with companies that make it policy to refuse to buy from companies that engage in illegal child labor in offshore locations, or that trade in conflict goods such as diamonds or gold used to support insurrections or genocide.

9. Contingency plans are critical for providers of outsourced services. How can client needs be served during power shortages, Internet shutdowns or slowdowns, or telecommunications problems on which much business hinges? Providers must be sensitive to the impact that terrorism and other risk factors, such as weather problems or pandemics, can have on their ability to deliver timely, quality service. They must therefore have good backup plans in cases of emergency.

10. The trend is to rely heavily on Far Eastern countries such as India, China, and others—including Malaysia and Thailand—for outsourcing. Regional outsourcing will continue as demand for outsourcing services for India and China outstrips their ability to deliver, which will mean that many countries in Asia can benefit from the high demand for outsourcing. Of course, one important factor is English, which is more readily spoken by workers in some Asian countries (India, Malaysia, Singapore, China, and the Philippines) than it is in others (such as Japan, Korea, and Vietnam).

Trends in Offshoring

Offshoring is commonly understood to mean moving work from one place or organization to another country to be performed. Much has been written about it in recent years. It thus overlaps conceptually with outsourcing, since sending work offshore often means outsourcing it as well. But offshoring can also mean closing entire facilities, such as industrial plants, in one country and opening them in another. In the latter case, the work is not outsourced; the organization simply moves its production or service delivery facilities from one geographical location to another.

Offshoring is usually done to take advantage of lower wage and benefit rates, different employment laws, and more business-friendly regulations in another country. An added benefit is that an organization may drive down its operating expenses through these methods while still selling products or offering services in nations where the price of goods is high. Organizations that offshore sometimes find that import/export trade policies, costs of transportation, and currency fluctuations can have major impacts on their businesses.

Trends in Insourcing

Insourcing has more than one possible meaning. First, it can mean moving work from an offshore location back to a domestic one.[2] A second possible meaning, less often used than the other, is to move work from one part of an organization to another part.[3] These alternative meanings do not have to be mutually exclusive, since it is possible to move work from an offshore location back to the United States but send it to a division, department, or work unit different from one that outsourced/offshored it initially.

As a simple example, suppose a U.S.-based corporation offshores its call center to India, and customer satisfaction measures fall significantly. The organization's leaders decide to bring the call center back to the United States, which would be one form of insourcing. But if a different corporate department were to be given responsibility for the new call center, that would be another form of insourcing.

Insourcing can occur when product or service quality is disappointing during offshoring, or when fuel prices rise so high that it no longer makes good economic sense to make something in one place and send it somewhere else. Alternatively, it could occur when one department is not as busy as another and leaders feel that work responsibilities would be better positioned in units with more slack.

Trends in the Geographical Movement of Work

Historically, much work has moved out of the developed economies of the world to the developing economies of China, India, and many others. Asia has been a preferred destination for the outsourcing and offshoring of work. There are many reasons why. Asia has huge labor forces, which means a huge possible base of consumers. Asia has a larger cadre of younger workers than is available in the "graying" economies of the West. Asian nations are known for having less onerous regulation of all kinds and more attractive taxation rates. Over the next twenty years, Asia will probably remain a preferred destination and a major engine of global economic growth.

But that will not always be true. Explosive business growth has prompted spot labor shortages in Asia. Turnover rates can be horrendous, averaging 100 percent annual turnover in an overheated economy like that of Vietnam. Labor mobility transcends national boundaries, too, with massive "brain drains" occurring from low-wage countries like the Philippines and Indonesia to higher-wage countries in the Asia-Pacific region such as Singapore, Hong Kong, and Australia. Well-qualified people, not always readily available in Asia, can sometimes command compensation packages that are equal to or that surpass those of their counterparts in the Western world. That trend is likely to continue, and retirees from Western countries may even be lured to Asia for new careers after they reach retirement age.

In the future, Africa may become a preferred source of labor,[4] provided the continent can overcome the challenges facing it, such as internal strife and widespread corruption.[5] While it is true that HIV and AIDS are a major challenge for the African continent, it is also true that the wage rates in that part of the world are by far the world's lowest (and thus the most attractive to employers). While it is true that low wages alone do not lead to job growth, low wages combined with stable, supportive governmental policies can be most helpful in attracting foreign investments as a kick start to job creation. Parts of Africa are also rich in raw materials necessary for manufacturing. There are 900 million possible consumers in Africa, making it a most interesting location for future economic growth. Look for the future of economic growth to shift gradually from Asia to Africa over the next twenty-five years as Asian economies move from "developing" to "developed."

Other Trends in Achieving Work Results or Staffing for Results

There are many unknown factors that could affect the future of achieving work results and/or staffing for results. Chief among these is the role technology can play.[6] *Assistive technology*, known best for its role in helping disabled workers perform work they could not otherwise perform, may have a broader role in the future. Two examples: (1) a computer that reads text aloud so that written language is accessible to those who are not sighted, and (2) a telephone that converts voice to text and back so that those without hearing can communicate by phone.

Assistive technology may have broader applications than its traditional use with the disabled. It may give employers the tools to shift the skills needed to achieve work results. Imagine the potential if, for example, a device could be created to provide immediate voice translations across languages or if an embedded chip could provide real-time work coaching from an expert to a novice. The day may not be far off when both of these dreams come true.

It is also entirely possible that a day may come when *nobody* ventures to work for a so-called full-time, permanent job.[7] Everyone may work by the task or by the project from home, linked together and linked globally by virtual aids such as instant messaging, videoconferencing, e-mail, virtual meeting spaces, and other technological support. Just as "virtual paper" may be growing cheaper than "real paper," virtual workers may end up being less expensive, and perhaps even more productive, when tapped on demand in the immediacy of real time to achieve work results. The boundaries between "work" and "personal life" could fall completely, to the point that work tasks will arrive virtually at any time, be completed and sent off virtually, and paid for virtually. Almost everyone may end up being a virtual worker responding to task bids through methods such as guru.com or elance.com. Even children may be schooled at home through online methods, a burden if parents go to work but more convenient than centralized brick-and-mortar schooling when parents work from home.

Of course, even in a virtual economy, there will always be exceptions to the rule. Some work simply cannot be effectively done virtually. Examples include individual healthcare and an array of personal services including manicures; haircuts; automotive repair; or the sales of "big ticket" goods such as automobiles, refrigerators, or washing machines. Although it may be possible to sell such goods virtually—it is easy, for instance, to simulate a test-drive of an automobile—many consumers actually prefer direct physical contact with what they may want to buy when the price is high and the quality of the actual good is essential to customer satisfaction.

Frequently Asked Questions and Tentative Answers

Question 1: What predictions can be safely made about the future of the workplace and workforce?

Answer: Full-time jobs may be going away, but work is not. In fact, work is becoming increasingly complicated and specialized. More work will be done in real time, using technology that makes instant and collaborative decision making across time zones possible.

Question 2: What final words of wisdom or advice would you, the authors, give future employers about how to get started in planning for future work and a future workforce?

Answer: Employers should experiment with ways of gathering precise metrics to assess customer and stakeholder needs, wants, and expectations for products and/or services. Employers will also need to do some market research to find out the essence of what makes their organizations competitive; that is, what makes their organizations better and different from their competitors, and how can they build on and leverage those strengths?

Question 3: What final words of wisdom or advice would you, the authors, give future workers about how to succeed in the future workplace and the future workforce?

Answer: We believe future workers will need to be very flexible and creative in how they can satisfy multiple clients or customers at the same time. In the future, the worker's fate—that is, future earning power—will not rest with one supervisor; rather, it will be affected by the individual's reputation for meeting or exceeding customer/stakeholder expectations. Learning ability (sometimes called learning agility) will be the key differentiator between the best and the merely average performers.

Question 4: What advice would you give government policy makers about how to address unemployment in each nation if you, the authors, are correct in your assumption that "jobs are going away but work is not"?

Answer: Countries like the United States spend huge sums of money on workforce development efforts to reduce unemployment. The problem is that policy makers continue to assume that the goal is to get everyone employed full-time. But that may not be the goal in the new economy. Instead, new ways of measuring employment may have to be devised that focus on earning power and what percentage of individual earnings goes for benefits. Government policy makers should also revisit traditional assumptions about how to estimate the demand for certain jobs or occupations, since work can be done in many ways apart from relying on full-time hires to do it. More attention should be paid to researching how work results are achieved and how people are used in an array of methods to meet work demands.

Question 5: What would you say will be the biggest challenge in dealing with virtual workforces?

Answer: Technology makes it possible to expect instant responses. But time zones and language/culture challenges will persist for the foreseeable future. Although a time may come when technology makes it easy to overcome language problems—such as translation software that is much more attuned to conceptual rather than literal translations—not everyone is available at all times and in all places. Recognizing that people may have to have "personal time" may be a big future challenge. Without some personal time, individuals may become more stressed in juggling the demands of multiple work providers.

Chapter Summary

This chapter examined the possible future of Lean but Agile work and workforce planning. It examined the future of a contingent workforce and trends in using such creative staffing approaches as outsourcing, offshoring, insourcing, and others (such as movements to Africa to take advantage of lower labor costs). Finally, the chapter ended by offering some final frequently asked questions—and their answers.

TALENT2 HUMAN RESOURCES PERFORMANCE AUDIT PROCESS FRAMEWORK

1. A human resource management performance audit can be a suitable method for evaluating the contribution of human resource activities to organisational objectives, assessed on the basis of value for money. It can identify areas where additional value can be obtained from an already valued, well regarded and award winning human resource department. The human resource management performance auditing methodology is set down in the Australian auditing standards (Standard on Assurance Engagements ASAE 3500) and assumes a professional practice framework for auditors.

2. Questionnaires assist in the collection of facts. An audit program is more comprehensive. Besides collection of facts, it also provides for their analysis in a systematic manner, although the audit does not extensively sample transactions. It is an Operational or Performance Audit, and concentrates more on systems and procedures rather than individual transactions.

Talent2 Pty Limited is the largest HR BPO service provider in the Asia Pacific. It provides an holistic service offering including HR advisory consulting and a range of best practice recruitment, payroll and learning solutions. http://www.talent2.com

Performance auditing is an independent, objective assurance and "consulting activity" designed to add value and improve an organisation's operations. It helps an organisation accomplish its objectives by bringing a systematic, disciplined approach to evaluate and improve the effectiveness of risk management, control and governance processes.

—(Institute of Internal Auditors—Standards)

Operational Auditing is a technique for systematically evaluating the effectiveness of a unit or a function in order to assure management that its aims are being carried out and to identify opportunities for improvement.

—Institute of Internal Auditors

Operational Auditing is a review and assessment of the efficiency an effectiveness of operations and operating procedures.

—Institute of Internal Auditors

Operational Auditing is applying good business practices, logical audit techniques and a management perspective to evaluate the organisation's objectives, operations, controls, communications and information systems. The auditor is concerned with the who, what, when, where, why and how of running an efficient and profitable business.

—Institute of Internal Auditors

Operational Auditing is a systematic process of evaluating an organisation's effectiveness, efficiency, and economy of operations and reporting to management the results of the evaluation along with recommendations for improvement. Its objectives are to provide a means for evaluating an organisation's performance and to enhance performance by making recommendations for improvements. Operational Auditing measures how well actual performance meets its measuring criteria, such as budgets, benchmarks, and other planning standards.

—Institute of Internal Auditors

The Auditing and Assurance Standards Board (AUASB) has released a new standard on Assurance Engagements, ASAE 3500 *Performance Engagements*.

Performance engagements assess the activities of entities in terms of their performance against established benchmarks: that is, the adequacy of internal controls, the extent to which resources have been managed economically or efficiently, and the extent to which the activities have been effective.

ASAE 3500: 12 The objective of a performance engagement is to enable the assurance practitioner to express a conclusion designed to enhance the degree of confidence of the intended users other than the responsible party by reporting on assertions, or information obtained directly, concerning the economy, efficiency or effectiveness of an activity against identified criteria.

ASAE 3500: 15 Ordinarily, performance engagements address a range of activities including:

- Systems for planning, budgeting, authorisation, control and evaluation of resource allocation.
- Systems established and maintained to ensure compliance with an entity's mandate as expressed in policies or legislation.
- Appropriateness of resource management.
- Measures aimed at deriving economies of scale, such as centralised resource acquisition, sharing common resources across a number of business units.
- Measures aimed at improving economy, efficiency or effectiveness.
- Appropriateness of the assignment of responsibilities, and accountability.
- Measures to monitor outcomes against predetermined objectives and performance benchmarks.

ASAE 3500: 17(h) "Performance engagement" means a performance audit or a performance review of all or a part of the activities of an entity (or entities) to assess economy, efficiency or effectiveness. It includes a "performance audit engagement" or a "performance review engagement" directed to assess:

(i)   the adequacy of an internal control structure or specific internal controls, in particular those intended to safeguard assets and to ensure due regard for economy, efficiency or effectiveness;

(ii) the extent to which resources have been managed economically or efficiently; and

(iii) the extent to which activities have been effective.

ASAE 3500: 17(d) "Criteria" in the context of a performance engagement means reasonable and acceptable standards of performance against which the extent of economy, efficiency or effectiveness of an activity may be assessed. Suitable criteria have the following characteristics:

(i) relevance: relevant criteria contribute to conclusions that assist decision-making by the intended users;

(ii) completeness: criteria are sufficiently complete when relevant factors that could affect the conclusions in the context of the performance engagement circumstances are not omitted. Complete criteria include, where relevant, benchmarks for presentation and disclosure;

(iii) reliability: reliable criteria allow reasonably consistent evaluation or measurement of the activity, including when used in similar circumstances by similarly qualified assurance practitioners;

(iv) neutrality: neutral criteria contribute to conclusions that are free from bias; and

(v) understandability: understandable criteria contribute to conclusions that are clear, comprehensive, and not subject to significantly different interpretations.

ASAE 3500: 18 In addition to the definitions included at paragraph 17 of this ASAE, the following definitions have the meanings attributed below. These definitions may have broader application in the public sector and should not be seen as limiting existing legislative arrangements or custom.

(a) *"Economy"* means the acquisition of the appropriate quality and quantity of resources at the appropriate times and at the lowest cost.

(b) *"Efficiency"* means the use of resources such that output is optimised for any given set of resource inputs, or input is minimised for any given quantity and quality of output.

(c) *"Effectiveness"* means the achievement of the objectives or other intended effects of activities at a program or entity level. It involves the assessment of outcomes.

ASAE 3500: 19 The assurance practitioner shall comply with the fundamental ethical principles of integrity, objectivity, professional competence and due care, confidentiality and professional behaviour.

In conducting the Audit, auditors should be independent and objective (IIA Practice Advisory 1100-1).

3. *Benefits/Outputs of an HR Performance Audit:*

- An accepted review methodology for Boards and CEOs

- A forward looking activity, focused on adding additional value

- A method for ensuring alignment between organisational goals and HR objectives

- A way of ensuring that management information and reporting systems are focused on providing reports on critical HR issues for organisational success and address key areas of interest for the Board

- A proven method for developing a 'value-for-money' culture within HR

- Recommendations will address whether the organisation's HR activities are being undertaken effectively, efficiently and economically

- Agreed action plans, accountability and timelines for recommended operational improvements

- Can be fully integrated with the organisation's internal audit program

- Enhances compliance with legislation, codes of practice and organisational policies and procedures

- A mechanism to properly articulate standards and agreed performance benchmarks in an organisational activity that is traditionally hard to evaluate

- A way of integrating a review of risk management, compliance and improvement within HR activity

Recommendations may be made for both improving processes and procedures, and strengthening controls.

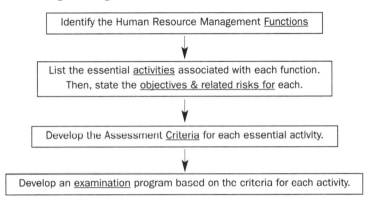

4. *The audit program framework:*

- What are the audit objectives?
- What are the audit criteria?
- What are the facts?
- Are there any deviations from the audit criteria?
- What are the causes of the deviation?
- What are the effects of the deviation?
- What are the risks associated with the deviation?
- What could management do to remedy the situation?

5. *Specify the Audit objective(s):*

5.1 What is the audit designed to achieve?

5.2 What are the questions the audit is expected to answer about the performance of HR and its respective focus activities?

5.3 What's important to the client?

5.4　The audit objectives may be influenced by what any previous audits or reviews highlighted as areas for improvement or change.

6. *Specify the Scope:*

6.1　Describes the parts or functions of the client that are and are not subject to the audit, in addition to the time period covered by the audit.

6.2　Is the audit to encompass all activity areas within HR?

6.3　Are there areas of high risk?

6.4　Which are the areas which may have the 'best' impact for improved performance, accountability or value for money?

7. *Risk Based Audit Methodology:*

Risk means the chance of something happening that will have an impact on the achievement of organisational objectives. Risk is measured in terms of consequences and likelihood. Risk management involves the systematic identification, evaluation and management of both risks and opportunities for business improvement, and is a key aspect of good corporate governance. This explanation is derived from the Australian and New Zealand risk management standard AS/NZ Standard 4360:2004.

The concept of risk includes the possibility of good things not happening (risk as opportunity), the threat of bad things happening (risk as hazard) and the potential that actual results will not equal anticipated outcomes (risk as uncertainty.)

We acknowledge that risk not only includes possibility of economic or financial loss or gain but also injury or death, physical damage, environmental harm, business interruption or a negative reputation and image.

Our risk based audit methodology is a process whereby potential threats to the client, its staff, or its operations are examined in a rational and clearly documented fashion. Risk assessment is typically undertaken to focus attention on significant audit areas, to allocate scarce audit resources to the most important audit areas.

During the planning phase of the audit, each identified risk is assessed as being Extreme, High, Moderate or Low. Risks assessed as Extreme, High or Moderate are generally included in the audit.

Factors other than risk may be taken into account and items identified as low risk may also be incorporated in the Audit. (For example, low risk areas may be specifically requested by the audit client)

Audit risks will differ according to the Audit type, but the process of risk identification and examination will be similar for all audit types.

The following table provides an indication of the types of risks to be considered when performing a risk assessment.

Strategic and Operational Risks	Are operational strategies appropriate to enable the Unit to meet its business objectives? What are the risks inherent in the processes that have been chosen to implement the strategies? How does the Unit identify, quantify, and manage these risks? How does it adapt its activities as strategies and processes change? Has the Unit developed key performance indicators to measure whether they have been successful in realising the perceived benefits of strategic objectives?
Financial Risk	Has the Unit succeeded in meeting measurable business objectives? What risks are related to compliance with regulations or contractual arrangements? Has the Unit incurred unreasonable liabilities to support operating processes?
Technology Risk	Are our information systems reliable? Do our systems meet business requirements? Are our security systems congruent with our technology strategy? Is the business relying on new, untested in production or outdated technologies including hardware, software and networks?
Knowledge Management and Information Risk	Are our data, information and knowledge reliable, relevant and timely? Is there an unreasonable dependency on temporary/contract staff? Are succession plans in place to enable knowledge and information transfer?

8. *Entry meeting with the client:*

Preparation occurs largely prior to the initial leadership meeting. However, this meeting may result in some amendments to the program.

8.1 Establish the communication protocols.

8.2 Identify key stakeholders.

8.3 Identify what's important to the client.

9. *The walk-through:*

9.1. Identify key staff to be interviewed during the audit.

9.2. Gain an understanding of the business/activity to be audited, identify the main areas of risk, and *validate the audit plan.* The review of background information could include:

9.2.1. Objectives and goals.

9.2.2. Results of other engagements, completed or in process.

9.2.3. Policies, plans, procedures, laws and contracts which could have a significant impact on operations.

9.2.4. Recent and/or imminent changes.

9.2.5. What are the activity's major risks?

9.2.6. What are their standards for monitoring performance?

The walk-through is a broad-based appraisal of the operations subject to audit, without carrying out detailed verification. The auditors gather information in order to fine-tune initial decisions about scope, cost, timing and skills, and to propose audit objectives, areas for in-depth review, criteria, and examination approach. In finalising these decisions, the audit team designs an audit to reduce the risk of making erroneous observations, faulty conclusions and inappropriate recommendations in the report to correspond with the level of assurance provided by the work.

10. *The engagement letter. This can be known as the terms of reference. It usually includes:*

10.1 The objectives of the audit;

10.2 The scope;

10.3 The methodology;

10.4 A list of recipients of the audit report;

10.5 The suggested time frame in which the audit will be completed.

Australian Auditing Standard ASA 210—*Terms of Audit Engagement* states that "The auditor and the entity should agree the terms of the audit engagement, which are to be recorded in writing by the auditor and forwarded to the entity."

11. *The Plan/the Audit program:*

The information above is reviewed with a view to identifying issues and areas to be covered within the audit. The auditor then designs a series of tests, procedures, activities and steps to collect evidence that will enable the auditor to report against the audit objectives.

This is a detailed plan of tasks to be performed during the audit, to guide its conduct and coverage. The audit program serves as a set of instructions to those involved in the audit, and as a means to control and record the proper execution of the work.

It demonstrates:

11.1 The risks to be assessed/the steps to be carried out during the audit.

11.2 How evidence will be gathered. (Section 12)

11.3 Standards/criteria against which the evidence will be evaluated, so that an audit opinion can be formed. (Section 13)

ASAE 3500: 32 The assurance practitioner shall plan a performance engagement so that it will be conducted effectively and achieves the objectives communicated or agreed in the terms of the performance engagement.

12. *Audit approach and methodology:* This comprises the techniques that will be used by the auditor in gathering evidence and conducting an analysis. Examples of gathering evidence include:

12.1 Review of the client's documentation, files, reports and studies

12.2 Conducting surveys

12.3 Interviews with staff

12.4 Intranet

12.5 Internet

12.6 Observation

13. *HR Standards/Criteria:* In evaluating the evidence, how can we identify what is right/good/better?

    13.1 Legislation

    13.2 Organisation policy

    13.3 Codes of practice

    13.4 Professional standards of practice (AHRI, Standards Australia)

    13.5 HEFCE (Higher Education Funding Council for England)

    13.6 Similar audit entities

    13.7 Comparison with similar entities (benchmarking)

    13.8 Expert panels

    13.9 Agreement between the auditor and auditee.

14. *Evidence:*

We desire to obtain sufficient evidence to be able to draw reasonable conclusions on which to base our opinions and provide valuable input to the client.[1]

Sufficiency is the measure of the quantity of audit evidence. *Appropriateness* is the measure of the quality of audit evidence, that is, its relevance and its reliability. The greater the risk, the more audit evidence is likely to be required and the higher the quality, the less may be required. Accordingly, the sufficiency and appropriateness of audit evidence are interrelated. However, merely obtaining more audit evidence may not compensate for its poor quality.

While recognising that exceptions may exist, the following generalisations about the reliability of audit evidence may be useful[2]:

    14.1 Audit evidence is more reliable when it is obtained from independent sources outside the entity.

    14.2 Audit evidence obtained directly by the auditor (for example, observation of the application of a control) is more reliable than audit evidence obtained indirectly or by inference (for example, enquiry about the application of a control).

    14.3 Audit evidence is more reliable when it exists in documentary form, whether paper, electronic, or other medium (for example, a contemporaneously written record of a meeting is more reliable than a subsequent oral representation of the matters discussed).

14.4 Audit evidence provided by original documents is more reliable than audit evidence provided by photocopies or facsimiles.

Audit planning and evidence gathering are influenced by *Materiality* and *triangulation*. Triangulation is the technique of investigating an issue by considering information on it from sources of different types. *"Materiality"* in the context of a performance engagement means variations of the measure or assertions from identified criteria for the evaluation or measurement of performance of the activity which, if omitted, misstated or not disclosed has the potential to adversely affect decisions about the economy, efficiency or effectiveness made by users or the discharge of accountability by the responsible party or the governing body of the entity. ASAE 3500: 17(g)

This work is then documented in working papers. In accordance with Auditing Standard ASA 500—*Audit Evidence* "The Auditor should obtain sufficient appropriate audit evidence to be able to draw reasonable conclusions on which to base the audit opinion."

ASA 230   Documentation states that "The auditor should prepare working papers that are sufficiently complete and detailed to provide an understanding of the audit. The auditor should prepare working papers that record the auditor's planning, the nature, timing and extent of the audit procedures performed, the results thereof and the conclusions drawn from the audit evidence obtained."

ASAE 3500: 76 The assurance practitioner shall prepare, on a timely basis, documentation that is sufficient and appropriate to provide: (a) a basis for the assurance practitioner's conclusion and Recommendations.

15. *Working Papers:* A template is provided as an Attachment to this Process Framework.

Typically, work papers will contain:

15.1 The audit plan.

15.2 Details of the audit work undertaken with conclusions noted.

15.3 Evidence that the audit work has been reviewed.

15.4 Summary of audit findings; their significance/risks; with associated draft recommendations.

15.5 Draft and final reports.

They should enable anyone not closely associated with the audit to follow the trail from objectives to findings to recommendations; to see what was done and what was discovered; to understand why the auditor concluded whether standards were met; and that the auditor's conclusions and recommendations are supported by the evidence and the relevant standards.

Audit working papers show that due professional care has been exercised and illustrate compliance with professional auditing standards. Careful documentation of work performed supports the findings, recommendations, and opinions contained in the final audit report.

16. *Comparison between Criterion and Condition = Finding:*

These are noted in the working papers, even when the Condition satisfies the Criterion.

The auditor must form and explicitly state their opinions/tentative conclusions about whether the criterion has been satisfied, and whether the *Issue* is likely to form part of the *Findings* in the Audit Report.

17. *Audit/peer review:*

Working papers should be reviewed, especially to confirm support for the observations and recommendations to be reported.

18. *Reporting to the Client:*

18.1 No surprises. During the course of the audit, it is regarded as good client management to keep the client informed about progress and findings so that, when the draft report is presented, there is no new information and no surprises. At the completion of field work an *exit interview* is held with management to discuss all significant matters arising out of the audit. The basis for the exit interview is generally a draft performance audit report. The exit interview:

18.1.1 provides an opportunity for clients to provide additional information, or correct any misinformation; and

18.1.2 serves to ensure that facts presented in the report are accurate and recommendations are appropriate, so that agreement is obtained to findings/recommendations and any due dates.

Exit interviews are to be offered, but may not be required if the auditor has been in regular contact with management concerning the identified issues, and the likely contents of the draft report. This contact would be evidenced by documentation such as File Notes.

ASAE 3500: 68 The assurance practitioner shall make the responsible party aware of:

(a) deficiencies in systems and controls; and

(b) variations of the measures or assertions from the identified criteria, that have come to the attention of the assurance practitioner and are material to the conclusions in the assurance report.

18.2 Structure of the Report:

18.2.1 Aims/objectives.

18.2.2 How was the audit conducted?

18.2.3 Who was interviewed?

18.2.4 Executive Summary.

18.2.5 Issues.

18.2.6 Risks.

18.2.7 Recommendations. The general guideline is that these are general and relatively broad.

18.2.8 Nominate responsible parties to implement the recommendations and due dates—which are negotiated, not imposed.

18.3 Cross referencing. The Audit report should be cross-referenced to the Working Papers, so that there is a clear linkage between the Issues raised in the Report and the Working Papers. In this way, the auditor's conclusions and recommendations are supported by the evidence and the relevant standards.

18.4 Draft. The draft report brings together the findings of the audit process. Ideally the report communicates these findings in a way that achieves the audit objectives that were outlined in the planning process. A report template has been developed to assist this process. The draft report is provided to the client following the completion of fieldwork, and its review.

18.5 Recommendations should have been discussed and, ideally, agreed at the Exit Meeting. Management then has an agreed time in which they specifically indicate their agreement or disagreement with each of the Issues and Recommendations. If there is disagreement, management will provide a rationale in their response to the draft report.

18.6 Final.

Professional Standards

- Australian Auditing Standards.
- International Standards for the Professional Practice of Internal Auditing—The Institute of Internal Auditors.

Bibliography

Andrews, C.J. (2007). *Developing and conducting a human resource management performance audit: case study of an Australian university.* Unpublished doctoral dissertation, University of Southern Queensland Toowoomba, Queensland.

Australian Universities Quality Agency (AUQA) (2008) *Audit Manual Version 5.* Retrieved 8 August 2008 from http://www.auqa.edu.au/qualityaudit/auditmanuals/auditmanual_v5/audit_manual_v5.pdf

Templates

19.1 File index for Work papers

19.2 Audit planning/Audit Program

19.3 File note and meeting note

19.4 Audit Issue Sheet

19.5 Draft report

19.6 Exit interview

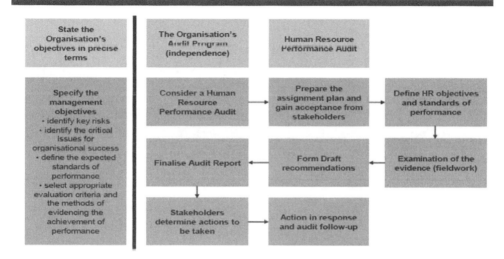

Human Resource Performance Audit

NOTES

Preface

1. William Bridges, *JobShift: How to Prosper in a Workplace Without Jobs* (Reading, Mass.: Addison-Wesley, 1994).
2. "Employer Costs for Employee Compensation," U.S. Bureau of Labor Statistics website, http://www.bls.gov/news.release/ecec.nr0.htm (accessed November 1, 2010).
3. "Say Goodbye to Full-Time Jobs with Benefits," CNN website, http://money.cnn.com/2010/06/01/news/economy/contract_jobs/index.htm (downloaded November 1, 2010).

Chapter 1

1. G. L. Johnson and J. Brown, "Workforce Planning Not a Common Practice, IPMA HR Study Finds," *Public Personnel Management*, 33, no. 4 (2004), 379–89.
2. Peter Cappelli, *Talent on Demand: Managing Talent in an Age of Uncertainty* (Boston: Harvard Business School Publishing, 2008).
3. American Management Association, *Survey on Downsizing, Job Elimination and Job Creation* (New York: American Management Association, 1996).
4. Benjamin Franklin to Benjamin Vaughan, July 31, 1786, Library of Congress, http://www.ledizolv.com/LearnAbout/LeadHazards/benfranklin.asp.
5. Courtney Rubin, "Employees are Unproductive Half the Day," study, March 2, 2011, http://www.inc.com/news/articles/201103/workers-spend-half-day-being-unproductive.html#.
6. D. Langdon, "Mind the Performance," *Performance Improvement* 49(8) (2010): 7–13. See also D. Langdon, *Aligning Performance: Improving People, Systems, and Organizations* (San Francisco: Jossey-Bass, 2000).
7. Langdon, "Mind the Performance."

8. P. J. Fadde and G. A. Klein, "Deliberate Performance: Accelerating Expertise in Natural Settings," *Performance Improvement* 49, no. 9 (2010): 5–14.

Chapter 2

1. Victorian Auditor General (VAG) (2010), "Performance Reporting by Departments," http://download.audit.vic.gov.au/files/Performance_Reporting_full_report.pdf (retrieved May 25, 2010).
2. Richard Boddington, personal communication, January 2011.
3. C. J. Andrews, "Developing and Conducting a Human Resource Management Performance Audit: Case Study of an Australian University" (2007), http://eprints.usq.edu.au/4297/ (retrieved September 30, 2008).
4. Higher Education Funding Council for England (HEFCE), "People Management Self-Assessment Tool" (2005), http://www.hefce.ac.uk/lgm/hr/selfassess/tool.htm (retrieved March 21, 2007).
5. Queensland University of Technology National Advisory Standards for HR in Australian Universities, http://www.hrd.qut.edu.au/hrbenchmarking/wpp.jsp (retrieved November 10, 2010).
6. http://www.referenceforbusiness.com/encyclopedia/Oli-Per/Organization-Theory.html.
7. http://www.kotterinternational.com/KotterPrinciples/ChangeSteps.aspx.
8. www.drjohnsullivan.com/articles-mainmenu-27/newsletter-archives.
9. http://abcnews.go.com/Travel/northwest-airlines-pilots-miss-airport-150-miles/story?id=8892976.
10. Watson Wyatt, *Competencies and the Competitive Edge*, Research Report, January 1998.
11. Aberdeen Group, November 2009.
12. Bersin Associates, *Talent Management Investments—Focusing on What Matters Most Through Talent Planning*. Research Bulletin 2009, Volume 4, Issue 19.
13. Watson/Wyatt 2008/2009 Global Strategic Rewards Report.

Chapter 3

1. Judith Hale, *Performance-Based Certification: How to Design a Valid, Defensible, Cost-Effective Program* (San Francisco: Jossey-Bass Pfeiffer, 2000).
2. John Holland, *Dictionary of Holland Occupational Codes* (Psychological Assessment Resources Inc., 1996), ISBN_0911907033.
3. Harry Brull, "Succession Planning and Talent Management: We've Come a Long Way, but . . . ," 2007 IPMAAC Conference, Personnel Decisions Inc., http://www.ipacweb.org/conf/07/brull.pdf.
4. Peter Cappelli, *Talent on Demand: Managing Talent in an Age of Uncertainty* (Boston: Harvard Business Press, 2008).
5. McKinsey & Company, Alumni–Dynamic Professional Network, http://www.quintiq.com/solutions/advanced-planning-and-scheduling.aspx.
6. McGladrey is the brand under which RSM McGladrey, Inc., and McGladrey & Pullen, LLP, serve clients' business needs. The two firms operate as separate legal entities in an alternative practice structure.

McGladrey & Pullen is a licensed CPA firm providing assurance services. RSM McGladrey provides tax and consulting services.

Chapter 6

1. Stacey Harris, "Talent Segmentation Within Your Company's Talent Strategy," Bersin & Associates, Research Bulletin, Volume 5, Issue 13 (2010).
2. Peter Cappelli, *Talent on Demand: Managing Talent in an Age of Uncertainty* (Boston: Harvard Business Press, 2008).
3. U.S. Department of Labor, "Employee Tenure in 2010." Bureau of Labor Statistics, USDL-10-1278, September 14, 2010. http://www.bls.gov/news.release/pdf/tenure.pdf.
4. Richard A. Ippolito, "Toward Explaining the Growth of Defined Contribution Plans," *Industrial Relations* 34, no. 1 (1995): 1–20.
5. Alistair Cockburn, *Agile Software Development* (Reading, Mass.: Addison-Wesley, 2001).
6. Jim Graber, "A Talent Management Success Story: How Veterans Administration Hospitals Became the Best," in *Government Succession Planning*, Case 10, ed. William Rothwell et al., pp. 109–38 (Amherst, Mass.: HRD Press, 2008).
7. Towers Perrin HR Services, "Winning Strategies for a Global Workforce" (2006), http://www.towersperrin.com/tp/jsp/hrservices_html.jsp?webc=203/global/spotlight/spotlight_gws.htm.
8. Bruce N. Pfau and Ira T. Kay, *The Human Capital Edge: 21 People Management Practices Your Company Must Implement (or Avoid) to Maximize Shareholder Value* (New York: McGraw-Hill, 2001).
9. Donald Vanthournout, Kurt Olson, and John Ceisel, *Return on Learning: Training for High Performance at Accenture* (Chicago: Agate, 2006).
10. ACT WorkKeys Work Readiness System Assessments, http://www.act.org/workkeys/assess/.
11. Cappelli, *Talent on Demand.*
12. Scott Adams, *Words You Don't Want to Hear During Your Annual Performance Review: A Dilbert Book* (Kansas City, Mo.: Andrews McMeel Publishing, 2003).
13. Peter F. Drucker, *The Practice of Management* (New York and Evanston: Harper & Row, 1954).
14. W. Rothwell, *Effective Succession Planning*, 4th ed. (New York: AMACOM, 2010).

Chapter 7

1. OrcaEyes, Inc. http://www.orcaeyes.com.

Chapter 8

1. D. McKenzie and M. Henderson, "Trends in Outsourcing Emerging from the Great Recession" (October 13, 2010), http://www.technologybar.org/

2010/10/trends-in-outsourcing-emerging-from-the-great-recession/ (accessed November 10, 2010).

2. M. Schniederjans, *Outsourcing and Insourcing in an International Context* (Armonk, N.Y.: M. E. Sharpe, 2005).

3. J. Galbraith, D. Downey, and A. Kates, *Designing Dynamic Organizations: A Hands-on Guide for Leaders at All Levels* (New York: AMACOM, 2002); T. Navarro, *Restructuring Your Organization: A Reorganization Guide* (Mountain View, Calif.: TGN & Associates, 2000); N. Stanford, *Guide to Organization Design: Creating High-Performing and Adaptable Enterprises* (London: Profile Books, 1996). For more information about how technology is changing organizational design and structure, see T. Malone, *The Future of Work: How the New Order of Business Will Shape Your Organization, Your Management Style and Your Life* (Cambridge, Mass.: Harvard Business Press, 2004).

4. V. Mahajan, *Africa Rising: How 900 Million African Consumers Offer More Than You Think* (Saddle River, N.J.: Pearson Prentice Hall, 2008).

5. G. Ayittey, *Africa Unchained: The Blueprint for Africa's Future* (Yarra Vic, UK: Palgrave-Macmillan, 2006).

6. See R. Donkin, *The Future of Work* (Yarra Vic, UK: Palgrave-Macmillan, 2009); A. McAfee, *Enterprise 2.0: New Collaborative Tools for Your Organization's Toughest Challenges* (Cambridge, Mass.: Harvard Business Press, 2009).

7. See W. Bridges, *Jobshift: How to Prosper in a Workplace Without Jobs* (New York: Da Capo Press, 1995).

Appendix

1. Auditing and Assurance Standards Board (AASB) (2006). *Auditing Standard ASA 500 Audit Evidence*. Retrieved 29 September 2008 from http://www.auasb.gov.au/docs/AUASB_Standards/ASA_500_28-04-06.pdf.

2. Ibid.

INDEX

ABOUT THE AUTHORS

William J. Rothwell, PhD, SPHR, is professor of Learning and Performance in the Workforce Education and Development Program, Department of Learning and Performance Systems, at The Pennsylvania State University, University Park campus. In that capacity, he heads up a top-ranked graduate program in learning and performance. He has authored, co-authored, edited, or co-edited three hundred books, book chapters, and articles—including seventy books. He is also president of his own consulting firm, Rothwell & Associates, Inc. (see www.rothwell-associates.com.)

Before arriving at Penn State in 1993, he had twenty years of work experience as a training director in government and in business. He has also worked as a consultant for more than forty multinational corporations—including Motorola, General Motors, and Ford. In 2004, he earned the Graduate Faculty Teaching Award at Pennsylvania State University, a single award given to the best graduate faculty member on the twenty-three campuses of the Penn State system. His train-the-trainer programs have won global awards for excellence from Motorola University and from Linkage Inc. His recent books include *Invaluable Knowledge* (AMACOM, 2011), *Competency-Based Training Basics* (with Jim Graber, ASTD Press, 2010), *Effective Succession Planning*, 4th ed. (AMACOM, 2010), *Practicing Organization Development*, 3rd ed. (Pfeiffer, 2009), *The Manager's Guide to Maximizing Employee Potential* (AMACOM, 2009), *Basics of Adult Learning* (ASTD, 2009), *HR Transformation* (Davies-Black, 2008) and *Working Longer* (AMACOM, 2008). He was a major researcher for the last three international competency studies of ASTD: *ASTD Models for Human Performance* (2nd ed., 2000), *ASTD Models for Workplace Learning and Performance* (1999), and *Mapping the Future* (2004). A frequent conference keynoter and seminar presenter in the United States and in many other countries, he can be reached by e-mail at wjr9@psu.edu.

James Graber, PhD, organizational psychologist, is managing director of Business Decisions, Inc., Chicago, Illinois, a company he founded in 1981. During his thirty years of consulting he has worked for more than a hundred domestic and international clients, including organizations such as McDonald's, United Airlines, Panasonic, General Motors, Abbott Labs, the U.S. Navy, and the City of Chicago, and for numerous clients in Australia, Europe, South America, Asia, and the Middle East. He specializes in the areas of competency modeling, talent and performance management, 360-degree multirater assessments, training needs analysis, employee development, career planning, succession, and workforce planning. Jim has directed development of talent and performance management software for more than twenty years, including the *focus* integrated talent-management software suite since 1995. He has taught at four universities and has had numerous publications, most recently *Competency-Based Training Basics* (with William J. Rothwell, ASTD Press, 2010), and conference presentations. Jim earned his bachelor's degree from the University of Michigan and his PhD in psychology from Claremont Graduate University in 1980. He can be reached by e-mail at jgraber@businessdecisions.com.

Neil McCormick has a broad history of international senior leadership experience spanning thirty-two years. Neil has worked in human resources and consulting services for the past seventeen years covering the spectrum of human resources activity. Neil has held a senior vice president position at Talent2, the largest HR BPO service provider in the Asia Pacific, since its inception. A recognized presenter and guest lecturer on the subject, Neil has a detailed understanding of, and passion for, the application of talent-management principles and processes for the ongoing success of business. Neil's latest development activity includes the creation of a Workforce Strategy & Optimization Consulting framework and Consulting Service to better align human resources to deliver the specific *objectives* of organizations. Neil is also an editorial advisor for *HR Examiner,* www.HRExaminer.com, and is an advisory board member of OrcaEyes Workforce Analytics Solutions, www.orcaeyes.com. Neil can be contacted by e-mail at neilmcc1@bigpond.com.